WHEN

HOLLYWOOD

WAS FUN!

[SNAPSHOTS OF AN ERA]

WHEN HOLLYWOOD WAS FUN!

[SNAPSHOTS OF AN ERA]

by Gene Lester
with Peter Laufer

A Birch Lane Press Book
Published by Carol Publishing Group

A Birch Lane Press Book
Published by Carol Publishing Group
Birch Lane Press is a registered trademark
of Carol Communications, Inc.

Editorial Offices: 600 Madison Avenue,
New York, N.Y. 10022
Sales and Distribution Offices: 120
Enterprise Avenue, Secaucus, N.J. 07094
In Canada: Canadian Manda Group, P.O.
Box 920, Station U, Toronto, Ontario
M8Z 5P9
Queries regarding rights and permissions
should be addressed to Carol Publishing
Group, 600 Madison Avenue, New York,
N.Y. 10022

Carol Publishing Group books are available
at special discounts for bulk purchases, for
sales promotions, fund-raising, or
educational purposes. Special editions can
be created to specifications. For details,
contact Special Sales Department, Carol
Publishing Group, 120 Enterprise Avenue,
Secaucus, N.J. 07094

Manufactured in the United States of
America
10 9 8 7 6 5 4 3 2 1

Library of Congress Cataloging-in-
Publication Data
Lester, Gene.
When Hollywood was fun!: snapshots of an
era/by Gene Lester with Peter Laufer.
p. cm.
"A Birch Lane Press book."
ISBN 1-55972-197-9
1. Motion picture actors and actresses—
United States—Portraits.
2. Hollywood (Los Angeles, Calif.)—Social
life and customs—Pictorial works. I. Laufer,
Peter. II Title.
PN1998.2.L47 1993   93–8846
791.43'028'092273—dc20   CIP

To my wife, Gloria, who for more than fifty years
had put up with my hobnobbing with the nuttiest people
and the most beautiful women in Hollywood

G. L.

BOB HOPE

I first met Gene Lester in 1935 when I was appearing in *Red, Hot and Blue* with Ethel Merman and Jimmy Durante.

I had just signed on with NBC for my first regular radio show and the network approached *Radio Guide* magazine to do a feature about me to publicize the new show. This was also during the early days of my marriage to Dolores. When the editors of *Radio Guide* tried to work up an approach to a story, Lester came up with the idea of doing it in the form of a picture layout.

Gene was one the first press photographers to use those new little 35mm cameras that today are the mainstay of the camera industry. With lenses faster than normal oversized press cameras, they could shoot in dimmer light and didn't need those disturbing flashbulbs that had just come into use.

The two-page picture spread showed Dolores and me out on the town at the Broadway hot spots like then then-famous French Casino and the Astor Roof. It was my first national magazine story and picture spread! All thanks to Gene.

In 1936 and '37, radio made its grand migration out west. Sound movies were *the thing* and Hollywood was gobbling up all the radio personalities it could induce to come west.

I signed with Paramount to do *The Big Broadcast of 1938*, and Dolores and I found a little house in the San Fernando Valley in an area called Toluca Lake. When Paramount set up a session for me to do a picture layout of us in our home, who do you suppose came out to do the assignment . . . Gene Lester. Gene was a free lance in those early days and only worked with top-rated magazines. The word in Hollywood was that if Gene Lester photographed you, those pictures would definitely get published. He was always on call to fan magazines and to the "biggies" like *Life* and *Look* and the *Saturday Evening Post*.

Then in 1942, when the motion picture industry sent out a trainload of movie stars to sell war bonds, they sent Gene Lester along to cover this month-long odyssey called the Hollywood Victory Caravan. Bing Crosby and I joined the group in Washington, D.C., and stayed with them for the rest of the tour. The Victory Caravan was the biggest war-bond selling effort put on by the movie industry.

In his more than sixty years covering radio, movies, and television, Gene has probably "shot" every star, bit player, producer, and director in the entertainment business. I recall seeing him at the Academy Awards, premieres, film locations, private parties, and just about everywhere celebrities would congregate.

Those were the days when Hollywood was not overrun by paparazzi, those free-lance photographers who now number in the hundreds and make it difficult for themselves and for us who now have to face them in hordes.

Since those early days, Gene Lester has been a fixture on the Hollywood scene and we have worked together for more than fifty years. Here is his life behind the camera — reflecting the good and the glitter, the fun and the beautiful of Hollywood. Enjoy.

GEORGE BURNS

After seeing Gene Lester's pictures, it brought back a lot of great memories. Hollywood was really fun in those days. I had lunch at my country club every day with some of the funniest comedians around. Sitting at what we called the Round Table were Groucho, Harpo and Chico Marx; Jimmy, Al and Harry Ritz; Al Jolson; Jack Benny; Danny Kaye; Georgie Jessel; and Lou Holtz, all trying to top each other. At the same table was Edward G. Robinson. He wasn't a comedian, but we needed someone to do the laughing.

They're all gone now; I'm the only one left. Now I'm the funniest one at the Round Table. I wish Edward G. Robinson was still around.

During all those Hollywood years Gene Lester was there with his camera taking pictures of Gracie and me, and all our fun friends. He must have been a great photographer, because I see the pictures they take of me now, and in the pictures Gene took of me fifty years ago I look much better.

George Burns

CHARLTON HESTON

Gene Lester stands tall among the still photographers who, over three generations, have captured the history of motion pictures as the art form of the twentieth century and, quintessentially, the American art form.

From the great days of the studio era into the expanding, kaleidoscopic spectrum the film industry has become, Gene was there with his cameras. He bears witness, not only with his gifted photographer's eye but with his succinct prose as to how it was and how it is . . . in the movies.

[CONTENTS]

WHEN

HOLLYWOOD

WAS FUN!

[SNAPSHOTS OF AN ERA]

GENE
LESTER AS
A SINGER
AT NBC.

Gene Lester lives in a modest, ten-room bungalow in the San Fernando Valley. Behind the house his garage has long ago been converted into an extended four-room workshop, office, darkroom, and storage room. The place looks a mess, with piles of photographs littering the desk and tables and an unmatched bunch of file cabinets filled with thousands of prints and negatives. There are publicity shots and other Hollywood mementos tacked to the walls and shelves. Cameras of all sizes are haphazardly dumped on tables and chairs, since Gene also happens to be the president of the American Society of Camera Collectors. A half-written letter sits curled in an old manual typewriter, while hundreds of reels of motion pictures line the shelves and lie stacked in the corners.

The man himself looks and acts a couple of decades younger than his eighty-two years. His eyes are clear, his memory is vivid, his language is punctuated with cuss words. When he tells his stories he has a tendency to descend into excruciating detail, but even he realizes this fault, sometimes catching himself digressing and then cutting to the chase. He conjures up, with fluency, famous names and their antics out of his past and tells his tales from memory. Sometimes an unimportant item from an incident he is recounting is left out, or he misses a date from a half-century ago by a year or two, or an inconsequential fact in a story is not quite accurate. For example, when he told me of his escapades on the set of *The Bride Came C.O.D.*, he remembered the plot as sending Jimmy Cagney flying Bette Davis through the night to the West Coast when in reality Cagney was off to Amarillo.

Such minor inconsistencies are of no importance as Gene spins his yarns. He brings to life — so brilliantly illustrated with his photographs — the excitement and fun of the good old days in Hollywood.

Gene approaches Hollywood with the enthusiasm of a super fan, but with the access of a working insider. It is a combination that results in a high-energy appreciation for his subject matter, but quite free of mindless star adoration. "I never looked at them as legends or as holier-than-thou people," he says now. "I'd say, 'Hey Clark [Gable] or Hey Chuck [Heston], I want you to do this.' I always acted like I was one of them rather than low man on the totem pole."

Gene Lester's brief biography: Born in Worcester, Massachusetts. Youngest son of county sheriff. During Depression could afford only two years at Boston University majoring in English and journalism to become a news reporter and photographer for Worcester and Boston papers. Sang around the house and serenaded girlfriend in canoes. Heard singing in canoe by vacationing opera star James Melton and sent to New York for audition on NBC.

Of that pivotal moment: "Only the laundryman knew how scared I was. I flopped miserably." Back to ten-dollar-a-month room until hearing about open auditions for Major Bowes on station WHN. "After hearing me sing, Bowes offered me a job as usher at the Capitol Theater on Broadway. Big letdown, but needing the money, I accepted." Two weeks later, put on the "Capitol Theater Family Hour" on NBC coast-to-coast as Bowes's latest discovery. Started meeting and working with the stars like Jack Benny, Ed Sullivan, Fred Allen, Burns and Allen. Began snapping celebrity photos. "I was one of the few guys in New York in those early days who used one of those new candid cameras, a Leica."

A full-page spread of Gene's early celebrity pictures was used in the New York *Herald-Tribune* which resulted in the radio show sponsors commissioning him to shoot their stars. Hired by *Radio Guide* magazine, he became its "singing cameraman," guesting on network shows and taking pictures for the magazine while the show was on the air. In 1937, when radio started to move to the West Coast, he and friend Marty Melcher (who later married Doris Day) drove out to Hollywood in an old Ford. For *Radio Guide* he sang on the Jack Benny Show, on "Hollywood Hotel" with Rudy Vallee, and on dozens of others. "I met publisher Moe Annenberg's son Walter at the *Guide* office. We were both very young and sat around the office with the rest of the staff having hamburgers. Little did I know that he would later become our ambassador to Great Britain," he says in a typical Gene Lester-style remark.

Once in Hollywood, Gene Lester spent the late thirties shooting for the fan magazines as a free-lancer, and in 1940 did a *Saturday Evening Post* assignment that kept him with the magazine for thirty years. He engaged in a variety of private productions and hustles to market his accessibility to the stars. The reward of this life's work is his hundreds of thousands of photographs, negatives, transparencies, and thirty hours of motion picture footage of Hollywood's Golden Age that fill his garage.

Most of Gene's peers are dead or do not own the rights to their work, and that's one of the reasons his collection is a treasure. The other — and probably much more important reason — is his style of picture taking. Even the contrived shots are not the stilted typical publicity shot. He prided himself in being a good director and making his subjects comfortable and appear natural. In addition, his collection includes thousands of outtakes from the assignments, the pictures that were never used and show the stars fooling around or are really candid shots. When the *Saturday Evening Post* went under, he signed with Twentieth Century-Fox to produce and direct documentaries on behind-the-scenes activities.

Gene Lester still enjoys poring through his files. He pulls out sexy fifties shots of Errol Flynn's companion Beverly Aadland at age sixteen for me to look at. "She had no boobs at all," his lasciviousness ever apparent. Then he launches into a detailed explanation of "cheesecake" and the wide variety of devices he and his colleagues developed to make the pictures they made of the stars appear sexier than real life.

In the darkroom, he's agile. He uses no timer, just estimating the needed time to print his pictures. His hot water for printing comes out of an old coffee pot. The room is a tangle of wires, trays, and chemicals. The sign on the door says, "This is a darkroom. Do not open the door or you will let out all the dark."

"Just name it, I've got it," Gene Lester says about his collection of Hollywood photographs, and it appears so. "I'm not rich," he says of his career, "But I've always been happy. I've had so much fun."

The quality of most of the images remains excellent. The years in the dry Southern California climate have been kind to them.

These are photographs that document a period when Americans often lived their dreams through the fantastic life of Hollywood stars. Gene Lester was there living that privileged life with them — and recording it for the rest of us. Now, these many years later, when the Hollywood of the thirties, forties, and fifties resonates in our country's collective memory with some Utopian innocence, Gene's pictures can be appreciated for their cultural value, as well as the thrill they offer to those of us continually fascinated by the Golden Age of Hollywood.

Peter Laufer
Hollywood, California
1992

My job was to tell a story in words and pictures about each star, how they did the normal things that the average person does. Did they wash their own clothes, or did they take them to the cleaners? Did they cook their own meals, or did they have a maid cook them for them? Did they dust their own furniture, make their own beds, and if they were the ones who made their own beds, I photographed them making their own beds.

The first thing I ever learned when I went to work for a Hearst newspaper back in Boston was never take photographs of snakes for Hearst papers, and never take photographs of deformed babies. Women readers turn away when they see that. When a snake comes out on television, my wife runs out of the room. They do not like to see those things. I see a picture of somebody vomiting in a movie and I ask, "Why?" You can always show a back view and hear a noise. You don't have to show the spew coming out like in that movie *The Exorcist*. The Hollywood mentality was different back in the old days.

We Hollywood photographers played by the rules. Our job was much different than that of a news photographer. We were part of the studio system, even those of us who worked as free-lancers, because Hollywood really was a company town in those days. Our job was to make the stars look good. Yes, we'd pry into their private affairs, but we never exposed their secrets. As long as we kept our noses clean we enjoyed regular access to the stars, because they knew we would keep their secrets and not take the kind of pictures that would reflect poorly on their lives and careers.

For example, if Bob Hope or Bing Crosby got involved in something for the war effort, they would let their publicist know. The publicist would call a photographer to go take the pictures, and that was where I came in. They would plant the shots in newspapers first, because if it was spot news, they would want it in the newspapers. If it was feature material, it would go into a magazine. I was hired in those types of situations by the publicist.

News photographers from the wire services or the newspapers would be invited to the formal, staged studio parties or staged publicity events. That was one device the studios used to maintain control. On a more important event like a private dinner party, the papers would not be invited.

The studios knew that we Hollywood photographers could be trusted. If a party turned wild, we would not shoot an actor going on the make, or whatever they did. Guys got drunk and did some pretty wild things at these parties, and it would have been unfair to take improper pictures.

The stars let their hair down in front of us because they trusted us. If a photographer loused up that trust, the studios and the publicists would stop hiring him. We would lose our access and consequently not have pictures to sell to our client magazines. There was no *National Enquirer* in those days.

The way I decided what to shoot and what not to shoot at private parties was simple. I asked myself: "Would I want someone to take such a picture of me?" Indirectly, these stars were paying for me to be there. There were no more than about a dozen photographers who covered the inside workings of Hollywood.

We were envied by the daily newspapermen because we would be invited to some personal events, whereas they would only be invited to the public stuff. That was how we got to know the stars well. Plus, I had another advantage. I was not originally a journalist. I was a performer myself. Some of these people knew me from the early days of my radio performing, when I was a singer.

I was almost in their class. I was never accepted completely, because I was a working man with a piece of equipment in my hand, and they were there all dressed up and fancy. At some of the parties that class separation bothered me. Here were people whom I had known, almost on an equal status, and now, all of a sudden, I was down there at the level of being a member of the working press and they were the royalty. But I realized that was how I was making a living. So be it.

Chapter One

When I went to Groucho's house to do a home layout for his radio show, I rang the bell and he opened the door. He looked at me and said, "Hello, I must be going." The old Groucho routine. Then he slammed the door in my face.

So I stood there and, after a bewildered pause, I rang the bell again. He opened the door again and asked, "What are you doing here?" — like: "I had told you to get the hell out of here!" I barged my way in and we started talking, and I found out that as nasty as he could be, he enjoyed people being nasty back to him. That was my first session with Groucho.

Years later, while I was illustrating his life story for the *Saturday Evening Post*, Groucho was vacationing out in Palm Springs. He asked me to come out there with my camera and spend the day. He said he would be out on the golf course and that he might have some friends come along.

Knowing Groucho's affinity for young girls, I hired four models who had worked for me and I told them we were going down to Palm Springs to see Groucho Marx. These girls were in shorts and tight sweaters and had great figures. On our arrival, Groucho came out and looked at me, and looked at the girls, and his jaw dropped. All the Marx Brothers were women chasers — Chico, Harpo, Zeppo, and Groucho even more.

Groucho could not take his eyes off the models. Working as my assistants, the girls helped me loosen Groucho up for the photo session and made him take me seriously as a working colleague.

Finally we went out to the golf links, and who do we meet there but Bing Crosby and Dean Martin. Harpo and Gummo Marx were there, too. They all piled on one golf cart. Dean Martin at that time had not had his nose job, so he looked like the

o Gene,
MN, YOU'RE GOOD!
GROUCHO

Italian guy that he was. He did not have that handsome profile. It was Lou Costello who financed Dean's nose job. They were good friends when Dean was just beginning.

So Groucho starts introducing the girls, and then he comes over to me and he whispers in my ear, "Are you screwing all these girls?"

I turned back to him and I said, "I'm not going answer that question, because if I told you I was, you wouldn't believe me, and if I told you I wasn't, you wouldn't believe me. And furthermore, it's none of your business!" That drove him crazy. He kept nudging me all that day to find out what was going on between me and the girls. He even put Bing up to asking me. But I still refused to answer.

Groucho bugged me for a year after that. One of those girls, Arlene Hunter, was a Marilyn Monroe look-alike. By that time, Marilyn Monroe was starting to make a name for herself.

WHILE PERFORMING AT A SAN DIEGO MARINE
BASE, GROUCHO WITH GUEST STAR GINGER ROGERS
AND HER HUSBAND, CAPT. JACK BRIGGS.

A PROOF
SHEET OF GROUCHO
ON "YOU BET
YOUR LIFE."

GROUCHO RAIDING
THE REFRIGERATOR
AT MIDNIGHT.
SOMETIMES WE
WORKED ALL
HOURS TO GET A
COMPLETE LAYOUT.

GROUCHO AND LUCY
CLOWNING FOR THE
CAMERA.

31

GROUCHO AND
WIFE NUMBER
THREE,
EDEN HARTFORD.

GROUCHO WITH THREE
OF MY MODELS IN
PALM SPRINGS.

ON THE GOLF CART: DEAN MARTIN
(PRE-NOSE JOB) AND HARPO ON *TOP*,
GUMMO, BING CROSBY, AND GROUCHO
ON THE *BOTTOM*.
THE STARLET ON THE *FAR RIGHT*
IS ARLENE HUNTER, WHO DOUBLED FOR
MARILYN MONROE.

GROUCHO
PLAYING
BASKETBALL
WITH HIS
SON, ARTHUR.

Chapter Two

T he first time I really got to know Jimmy Stewart was when we were on a train ride to Santa Fe. Warner Brothers staged the premiere of the Errol Flynn movie *Santa Fe* up there and the studio chartered a train and loaded it with stars and the press for a three-day holiday.

We were on our way home on the train through a blinding snowstorm, and between Albuquerque and Williams, Arizona, the train stopped. We knew of no reason for us to be stopped. They put us on a siding and the next thing I knew, Olivia de Havilland was rushed to the hospital in one of those little towns near the Grand Canyon. I thought, "Wow, if Olivia de Havilland has been sent to the hospital, I want to find out where, and get a picture of her."

Getting off the train, I found a sleigh. I could not go by car because the snow was so heavy. A sleigh ride was the best way to get to the hospital.

Arriving there, I managed to get into Olivia de Havilland's room and who do I find with her but Jimmy Stewart. Nobody had ever suspected that there was ever a romance between them. But at least for the fan magazines, this was a twosome that was unusual and when would you ever get a picture of them in a hospital? Jimmy was sitting there just having a conversation. They greeted me pleasantly and I shot some pictures of Olivia with Jimmy sitting there beside the bed. Evidently, Olivia had developed a female problem that required immediate attention.

In that heyday of radio, Jimmy would do a lot of appearances, as a guest star on "Lux Radio Theater" and other network dramatic shows. The *Saturday Evening Post* sent me out to do a home layout of Jimmy and show him with some of his friends, such as Hank Fonda and Gary Cooper. At his house, I met his wife Gloria, whom he had

married since the train trip, and their twin girls. We spent several days working together at his home in Beverly Hills.

On one of those days, he invited Gary Cooper to come over. Remember, Jimmy Stewart was the quiet, stuttering type who would say, "W-A-L," really drawing out the word slowly. And Gary Cooper was the silent type of a cowboy who would say, "Yup," and that's it. So in his living room, Jimmy had one of the biggest sofas I had ever seen, it must have been ten or twelve feet long. I decided to put Gary Cooper on one end and Jimmy Stewart on the other, both with their feet in cowboy boots up on the coffee table. When I captioned the picture, on one side I put "W-A-L" and on the other side I put "Yup" and then I added, "This was a two-hour conversation."

ALTHOUGH STEWART WAS ALWAYS
THIN, I FREQUENTLY FOUND
HIM NOSHING.

AFTER SHOWING SOME HOME MOVIES ONE NIGHT,

STEWART REACHED FOR HIS ACCORDION

AND STARTED PLAYING SOME COUNTRY SONGS.

HE PLAYED WELL, AND SANG WITH AN OFF-KEY VIBRATO.

GARY COOPER ON VIOLIN
DURING A CBS RADIO REHEARSAL.
JOAN LESLIE AND
WALTER BRENNAN WATCH.

ON LOCATION NEAR LOS ANGELES AT THE DISNEY RANCH, COOP AND DIRECTOR WILLIAM WYLER DISCUSS AN UPCOMING SCENE.

GARY COOPER
AND HIS
MOTHER.
MRS. COOPER
WAS PRESIDENT
OF THE MOVIE
STARS
MOTHERS'
CLUB.

GARY COOPER
WAS A
CARTOONIST
FOR HIS
HOMETOWN
MONTANA
NEWSPAPER
BEFORE COMING
TO HOLLYWOOD.
HERE HE
WATCHES HIS
ART STUDENT
DAUGHTER
MARIA AT
WORK.

COOPER MAKING MOVIES OF HIS MOTHER. *TOP*

DAUGHTER MARIA AND WIFE ROCKIE
JOIN GARY AND THE DOGS FOR A WALK IN FRONT
OF THEIR HOME IN BRENTWOOD. *CENTER*

COOP AT HOME WITH HIS MOVIE CAMERA
READY FOR ACTION. *BOTTOM*

Chapter Three

My only run-in with a studio happened in a most unusual way. My friend, movie director George Sidney, and I were at the Beverly Hills Hotel pool one Saturday afternoon. We had stopped by as that was the hangout for the young movie crowd and we thought we'd run into Bob Stack or Jackie Cooper or perhaps Betty Grable.

Instead we ran into MGM star Norma Shearer, who was with director Edmund Goulding and a cameraman as they were trying to shoot inserts for her film *The Women*. I knew Norma from having photographed her at parties with her husband, Irving Thalberg, who was one of the studio's major executives in those days.

At Goulding's direction, Norma removed the robe she was wearing, revealing a tight, figure-clutching bathing suit. An exclusive picture in a swimsuit would have been a feather in my cap with my magazine editor, so I borrowed George Sidney's Rolleiflex (in which he had a fresh roll of film) and ran over to where Goulding and she were working. Before I reached them, Norma bent over and threw her legs up in the air. This made even a better shot — Norma standing on her head in a bathing suit. She and Goulding agreed to let me shoot and I killed the whole roll of film with exposures of the event. Then on Monday morning I got a call from Howard Strickling, who was the head of publicity at MGM.

"Gene Lester?" he said to me, "You took some pictures of Norma Shearer in a bathing suit standing on her head."

I said "Yes! She looked great."

He was not amused and ordered, "I want all those pictures killed."

"What?" I said. "What? What was wrong? She looked great."

"She is the wife of the head of production here at MGM," he came at me sternly, "and I want all those pictures killed." He went on for several minutes. "If you

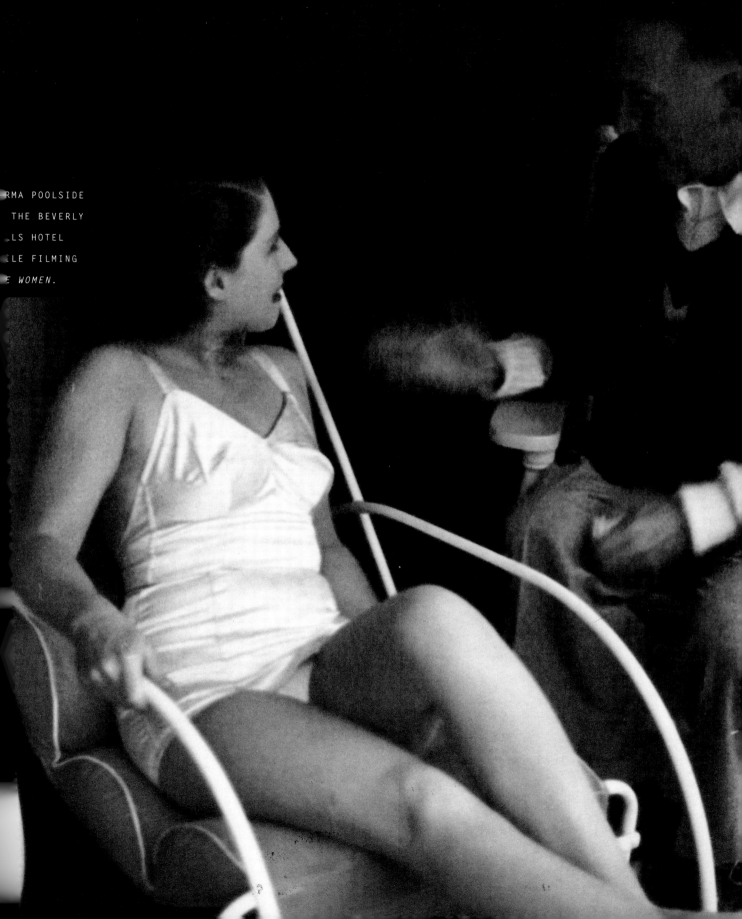

RMA POOLSIDE
THE BEVERLY
LS HOTEL
LE FILMING
E WOMEN.

don't kill them, if you run those pictures, we'll see that you never work at MGM again. In fact, you'll never be able to shoot pictures in Hollywood anymore."

"Howard," I was so puzzled. "What's wrong, what could be so wrong with this?"

He just replied, "I don't care, we want those pictures killed. Every shot you made!"

So I said, "Well, Howard, since this sounds like it's going to be a big problem, I think I'll call my very good friend in Atlanta, Col. Ed Schiller."

"What?" he sounded shocked. "You're a friend of Ed Schiller's? You know Ed Schiller?"

Ed Schiller was a friend of Louis K. Sidney, who was the father of George Sidney and a vice-president of MGM. I used to work for Louis K. Sidney in New York when I was a radio singer at WHN, the MGM Loews Theater station. Colonel Schiller came up from Atlanta, Georgia, to visit Louis K. Sidney, and he had bought a Graflex camera in New York and did not know how to use it.

Louis K. Sidney called me into the office and introduced me to Ed Schiller, and asked, "Gene, do you know how to work this camera?"

I said, "Sure, I used to use it when I worked for the *Worcester Telegram* up in Massachusetts when I was in high school."

Sidney asked, "How would you like to teach Ed Schiller how to use his Graflex?"

I had a dark room around the corner from Loews State Theater, where the radio station was, so I took Ed Schiller there and I explained how his camera worked. As a result Schiller and I became close friends. I even visited him once on a trip to Atlanta.

Col. Ed Schiller happened to be one of the biggest stockholders in Loews Incorporated, the holding company of Metro-Goldwyn-Mayer. Anything Schiller said seemed to be law at Loews Incorporated and at MGM. The mention of Ed Schiller after I took the Norma Shearer shots put a whole new attitude into Howard Strickling.

I had lunch with Howard Strickling the following day and he said, "Well, Gene, I'll tell you, since you're one of the MGM family, it'll be okay. Go ahead. Use one picture in your magazine. But be very careful. Use the nicest one. And please do right by Norma."

That was my only experience with that type of an operation. The studios controlled their contract players. The studios could even blackball photojournalists in Hollywood who refused to play by the rules they set.

Chapter Four

O ne day I bumped into Errol Flynn. I had known him from Warner Brothers, but only casually.

He came over to me and said, "Gene Lester, I have got to shake your hand."

"Why?" I asked.

"Well," he answered, "you happened to date a girl that I've been trying to date for the last six months. And she's always turned me down. For that I have to shake your hand. They say all girls chase me. You're the only guy I know who has beaten me to a date with a girl that I was after. So anytime you want me to do any favors for you, for your magazines or anything, call on me. I'm your friend."

I thanked him and I said, "Well, look, Flynn, I'm doing a movie short which I'm trying to sell to your studio, Warner Brothers."

I called it *Peeks at Hollywood* and it dealt with two young pretty girls who go up to the Griffith Park Observatory overlooking Hollywood. They put a dime in one of those tourist telescopes and point it around. Then they point it at a house and spot a star.

I figured if Errol Flynn would do a sequence in this show, that would make Warners buy it. When Flynn said he would do it, I flipped.

He had a Packard convertible with a special body. They called it a Darrin body. Flynn is shown in the last sequence of the film driving in to the studio gate. He gets out of his car with script in hand and walks over to the door of the stage where he is supposed to be working. As he goes to open the door, the red light goes on. A sign says, DO NOT ENTER WHEN RED LIGHT IS FLASHING.

He stands there awkwardly and looks around. First he looks at the script. Then he looks up at the sky, and when he does, he reacts as though he sees the two girls.

He waves up to the girls and they start waving back at him. Flynn points at the

script and makes like a movie, and points at the door, and when we get the door in the shot, he turns to the girls and he motions, "Come on down, I'll take you in and you'll watch the movie being made."

Just as that is happening, and he is ready to enter the soundstage, the telescope goes black and a sign says, "Your time is up; another ten cents please." The girls go looking for another dime and they dump everything out of their purses. But they do not have another dime. We "iris out" on the two girls sitting there, forlorn and crying. That was the end of the short.

Jack Warner called me in and demanded, "What the hell are you doing with our star, Errol Flynn? What did you have to pay Errol Flynn to do that?"

I said, "I didn't have to pay him anything. He offered to do it as a favor."

Warner said, "You mean Errol Flynn signed a contract with you without getting paid? If we brought him into the studio to scratch his butt or to blow his nose, we'd have to pay him ten thousand dollars." Jack Warner bought my short for twenty-five hundred dollars, a good price in those days.

That was how the studios controlled their people. They were not supposed to do anything for anybody else. But some would work with you on a friendly basis. They did you favors, because they knew that their careers depended to a degree on how well Hollywood press people treated them with photographs and in print.

The girl I took out on that date, the girl that Errol Flynn wanted, was a hatcheck girl at a nightclub on the strip who worked until two in the morning. I happened to walk in at 1:30 the night of her birthday and she had no one to celebrate with.

HERE, FLYNN
IS JOINED
BY OLIVIA
DE HAVILAND.

Chapter Five

Around 1939, Howard Hughes decided to make a movie called *The Outlaw*. He signed a new girl, I think she had been a dental assistant. Howard hated photographers because they always grabbed pictures of him when he least wanted them to. There were a few of us who, whenever we would see Howard, knew that he did not want his picture taken, so we would put the camera to the side. Howard appreciated this and when *The Outlaw* was being made asked for a bunch of the photographers he liked to go up on location in Moencope, Arizona — which is on the fringes of the Grand Canyon in the Hopi Indian Reservation — and photograph Jane Russell and Jack Buetel on location.

Hughes's publicity man, Russell Birdwell, called us all aside and told us, "Howard just signed a girl with the biggest chest in Hollywood. We want her boobs publicized. We don't care how you do it, just as long as you get her cleavage showing."

The location was a tent city in the desert on the Hopi Indian Reservation. In each tent they had a little propane heater for the cold nights out there. When we arrived, all the photographers and the publicity people got together and realized someone had to tell Jane what Howard wanted us to get from her.

Birdwell said, "I'm too embarrassed to go over and ask her. Who wants to talk to Jane?"

Nobody volunteered, so we drew straws. I was the littlest guy there, I was the youngest guy there, I was new in Hollywood, so just my luck, I drew the assignment.

I did not know how to go about it, so I thought the only thing I can do is come right out and blurt it out. Why beat around the bush? It would embarrass me; it would embarrass her. Confronting Jane, I blushed and stammered. She seemed unfazed and just said, "What do you want me to wear?"

"The best thing I can think of," I burbled, "is a nightgown that's low in front."

She put one on and you could almost see through it, it was so sheer. I got some shots of her leaning over brushing her teeth, on the floor lighting the heater—anything to get her to lean over where you could look down her cleavage.

We spent four or five days on location up there and wherever she happened to be we had to have cleavage. For one of the shots she was washing her stockings leaning over the toilet bowl. But for my best shot I had Jane in her nightgown stand on the bed. The tent fortunately had a high ceiling, and she started jumping on the bed just like on a trampoline.

"Jane," I said to her, "when you get up at what you feel is a high peak, just throw your legs up too." I shot a picture of her flying through the air and it turned out beautifully.

Chapter Six

I knew Dinah Shore in New York when her name was Fanny. I used to sing on WHN in New York and with Major Bowes on the "Capitol Theater Family Hour." This was when I was twenty-three years old, fresh out of Worcester, Massachusetts.

I worked as a photographer with Dinah when she got into television on the Chevrolet show. During the war, I was in the army, stationed in San Pedro at Fort MacArthur. Because I had to come into Hollywood regularly to buy photo supplies — I was the fort photographer — the major in charge of my operation used to give me a whole book of passes, all pre-signed, and all I did was fill in the time.

I would write passes for myself and come home every single night. I convinced Dinah to come down to the base and do a show for us and it set me up at Fort MacArthur. The fact that I knew Hollywood celebrities made me a hero. She was one of the top vocalists of the time; it really made a big impression at the fort when this little buck private could bring in people like Dinah Shore.

Lou Costello was instrumental in getting the colonel to keep me at Fort MacArthur. He had gone to the colonel on my behalf and said, "You keep Private Lester here at Fort MacArthur and as long as he's here, I'll come down with Bud Abbott and do all the shows you want us to do." And he did.

Dinah was so gracious about this sort of activity. She was always the lady. Dinah was never what you call a tough broad, like Madonna is today, or that Sinead O'Connor with a bald head who tore up the Pope's pictures. Dinah was a perfect lady. You could not ask for a nicer person. Strangely enough, although she was not the most beautiful person in the world, she photographed well.

DINAH SHORE AT
THE PIANO, GRACIE
ALLEN ON FIDDLE,
PAUL WHITEMAN
BELTING OUT
THE SONG.

DINAH
TRYING
TO LOOK AT
HOME IN THE
KITCHEN.

Chapter Seven

I first met Jimmy Cagney in 1939 when he made a movie with Bette Davis in Death Valley called *The Bride Came C.O.D.* He played an airplane pilot delivering Bette Davis from New York to her fiancé on the West Coast. On the way across country, in a single-engine plane, they crashed in Death Valley. In the script he and Bette Davis got into a fight and she threw him into a cactus plant.

The cactus plant was not real; it was a rubber plant made by the prop department at the studio. But the publicity office at the studio sent out a story that Jimmy Cagney had been thrown into a cactus plant during filming in Death Valley and had 275 cactus needles sticking into him. The story they planted explained that the film crew pulled out all those needles.

That story ran all over the world. I was there and took the pictures of Jimmy in the rubber cactus plant. Then for my purposes I had him throw Bette into it as well. Everyone on the set had a ball sitting their butts into the phony cactus for a snapshot.

Once on the set at the Warner studio early in the forties, I was there taking pictures of Jimmy. He was on a horse and wagon and William Keighley was directing the production. Here was a good Irish director with Jimmy Cagney, a nice little Irish actor. I was behind the camera, with a Rolleiflex.

When Keighley yelled, "Cut!" Jimmy stood up in the wagon and let out some comment in Yiddish. And nobody said anything. They didn't understand. Standing there, I knew what he said, so I yelled back to him in Yiddish. What I said was, "Vos hakst du zay a chynick," which roughly translates to "Why are you bothering them a teakettle" and really means "Stop talking nonsense."

He looked down and asked, "Who said that in Yiddish?" I answered him in Yiddish, and he started speaking to me in Yiddish. Then he got down off the wagon

CAGNEY
CS AMONG
RUBBER
US IN
H VALLEY.

and came over to me, talking in Yiddish. I was talking back to him in Yiddish, and the rest of the crew was standing there gawking at the two of us. Nobody knew what the hell we were talking about.

After that day, every time I saw Jimmy Cagney, we only spoke Yiddish. We never spoke any other language between us, and Jimmy loved it. "When I was a kid," Cagney explained, "I was living on the East Side of New York, and all the Jewish people were living around us. The meat market was Jewish, the grocer was Jewish, the baker was Jewish, the tailor was Jewish, everybody was Jewish. My family had to have somebody in the family who could speak to these people, or we couldn't have bought anything. We couldn't have bought groceries, we couldn't have had our laundry done; they didn't understand English. They were all immigrants who had just come over. So I learned Yiddish because I was the youngest one and I was more adaptable to learning at the time than my older brothers."

Few Hollywood fans know that Jimmy Cagney was great on the guitar. Whenever he was off the set he used to sit noodling on his guitar. Jimmy was a great guitar player. I had to sneak pictures of him playing the guitar, because he didn't want anyone around to bother him.

In Death Valley when he was making *The Bride Came C.O.D.*, I went into his tent during a break in the shooting, and Jimmy was sitting there with his guitar. I had a miniature Speed Graphic on my lap. About half the size of the press camera, the Speed Graphic took film sheets that were only two-and-a-quarter by three-and-a-quarter.

Jimmy was sitting there noodling away, and I thought, "I must get a picture of this, but I dare not use a flash because it would disturb him." Jimmy was tough. His temper would come fast. I did not want to bother him or make him angry.

I looked at him. My thoughts rambled, "The light is coming through the open flap of the tent and it is lighting just half of his face. He's studiously playing on his guitar, a twenty-fifth of a second at F4.5." I left the camera on my lap, I turned the diaphragm to wide open, set the shutter at a twenty-fifth and cocked it, then I figured he was four-and-a-half or five feet away from me, I leaned back a little and made the setting five feet. I kept the camera in my lap, and tried not to do anything that would make him think that I was taking a picture. Finally, I took the cable release in my hand.

Of course once the shutter snaps it makes a pretty loud noise, but I employed a trick always used when I was trying to take pictures without the subjects knowing. I coughed, so that while the camera clicked, the sound was overpowered by my cough.

Nobody pays attention to a cough. They do not look and see what is going on if you cough. But they will look up and say, "What the hell are you doing?" if they hear the click of a shutter.

I got a shot of Jimmy that is really a classic. I couldn't have done better in my studio. The lighting is so great. His attitude and his face are so good. It is one of my prize photos. To this day, I look at it as one of my favorites.

Chapter Eight

When I was in high school, I fell in love with Joan Crawford. So the first time I met her, I was completely astonished by the number of freckles she had. Her face was covered with so many freckles that I could not believe it, because I remembered back in high school seeing a movie where Joan Crawford got up in front of everybody on a yacht and took her clothes off, down to her underwear, and dove into the water. To me, that was one of the sexiest shots I had ever seen on the screen.

Finally meeting Joan Crawford, and seeing her with all those freckles on her, I could not figure out how the photographers could disguise them. But it was all due to the skill of the makeup department.

When *Silver Screen* asked me to go out and do a home layout on Joan Crawford, I just loved the idea, because this would give me the chance to get to know her better.

When Joan came downstairs to meet me, she came over and put her arms around me and gave me a kiss on the cheek. Wow! This was like being in heaven. A girl that I dreamt of as a youth, and here she was in person. I was in her living room and she gave me a kiss!

We went through the photo session with her adopted daughter. She wanted to have her daughter in the pictures because they had on identical outfits. They had mother-daughter outfits. It was a very hot afternoon and she suggested, "How would you like to take some pictures in the pool? In fact, how about going swimming with me?" Egad! What an invitation!

"I don't have any bathing trunks," I said.

"Oh," she said, "I've got a lot of men's trunks, and don't worry, they've all been laundered."

I said, "Fine," although I couldn't swim. But I could not pass up an opportunity

CRAWFORD
ER DAUGHTER
TINA,
AUTHOR OF
DEAREST.

to get into a pool with Joan Crawford. This was something you write home about. That day I happened to shoot a picture of Joan that I love. She is hanging on to the diving board, and I am standing on the diving board, looking down at her in the water, and my white shoes are in the picture. That is my favorite picture, although later I did get some shots of me in the pool with her.

Howard Strickling, the publicity man at MGM, had told me I was required to send him the negatives so that they could be retouched because her freckles, all over her shoulders, her chest, her back, were so unbelievable. But I was convinced her freckles could look appealing if the photographs were properly exposed.

I said to Joan, "You know, Howard doesn't believe that I could make you not freckly, looking as if you have some bad skin problem with all these dots all over you. But I'm convinced that I can make you look so good that you may like to see yourself in the freckles."

She said, "Look, if you want to try it, I want to see them first. I want to look at all the pictures, and I want Howard to look at all the pictures you take. If we disapprove of any of them, you have to tear them up and destroy the negatives."

"That's fair enough," I said. "As long as you give me the chance." I had a technique where I slightly overexposed negatives, and when I printed them, I would not print them on contrasty paper, I printed them on soft paper, because the blacks were very black on the negatives, so the paper would accept it. I shot with a 35mm camera and I never made prints bigger than five-by-seven. In a five-by-seven print, nothing would be as blatant as it would be in an eight-by-ten or in an eleven-by-fourteen. I printed the entire roll of her, with her freckles, on soft paper.

I showed the whole batch to Joan and to Howard Strickling and Joan said, "These are the first pictures I've ever seen where my freckles show and I don't mind. People know I've got freckles. But I don't like them when they're black splotches all over me. I don't mind if they're visible, but not if they're coming at you like the gorilla that ate Brooklyn."

It was that assignment with Joan Crawford that opened the door for me to use a 35mm camera on more Hollywood shoots. In those early days, the female stars had to be photographed with four-by-five film so that there was enough area for retouching. 35mm is almost impossible to retouch. Today, with improved lenses and films, almost every Hollywood photographer uses 35mm. Fifty years ago that was a no-no.

Chapter Nine

I met Judy Garland in New York when she was twelve years old. Her last name was Gumm, and she and her mother were guest stars at the Ziegfeld Theater in New York on a WHN radio show. Judy had been tested by MGM and signed a few months earler, but she was introduced to me as Judy Gumm.

Around 1937, Judy Garland was making the Andy Hardy movies at MGM with Mickey Rooney. I used to go to a lot of functions in Hollywood in those days as a fan magazine photographer. We photojournalists would not only cover the parties, the studios would have get-togethers and social events that also were open to those photographers who maintained good relationships with the stars. Judy Garland and other young performers would be at many of these and a lot of times we would do kid layouts for the fan magazines: what the young stars in Hollywood were doing.

For example, I remember taking Judy and Jackie Cooper out to the Sportsmen's Lodge. It had just opened in the San Fernando Valley and they featured a bowling alley there. Judy and Jackie Cooper were bowling and I took some action photographs of the two. As a gag, Judy held up two big bowling balls in front of her chest and Jackie Cooper put his arms around her from behind. He was laughing because here she was with these great big balls looking like her boobs.

JUDY AND GENE KELLY
ON DICK POWELL'S
RADIO SHOW, TRYING
TO DEAL WITH
HIS SAXOPHONE
PLAYING.

JUDY GARLAND
DANCING
ONTO BOB
HOPE'S RADIO
STAGE WITH
JERRY COLONNA.

JUDY GARLAND
WAS EIGHTEEN
WHEN SHE MARRIED
CONDUCTOR DAVID ROSE.
I AM THE PHOTOGRAPHER
ON THE FAR RIGHT,
SHOOTING FOR
SILVER SCREEN.

Chapter Ten

I first met Marilyn Monroe when she was Norma Jean Doherty. She was married to a Van Nuys policeman and on the verge of breaking up with him. She was handled by a model agency called the Blue Book Agency, run by a woman named Emmaline Snively. At that time, Blue Book had taken an office two doors away from mine, a store on Vine Street off Sunset Boulevard. We were practically next door to each other.

Snively sent this girl, Norma Jean Baker, up to me. She did not look like the class model that you would see in *Vogue* or *Harper's Bazaar*. To me she looked like just an average cheesecake-type model. She came into the office and I was not too impressed. We took her vital statistics and kept them on file. Snively evidently advised her to hang around my office, because I was doing a lot of commercial and advertising photography, along with my magazine work.

So Norma Jean used to come up and sit around for hours to see what was going on and wait for an assignment. I paid no attention to her, because she was down in the front office and my studio was up a flight of stairs. She would sit in the reception area and the guys working for me would all come over and say, "Who's the broad? Who's the broad? Wow. Get a load of her." She always wore some kind of a tight dress or sweater that showed off her bust.

One day we received a call from Clairol saying that they needed a blonde, a brunette, and a redhead for a new advertising campaign. Clairol executives were coming out from New York to supervise the photography.

I called Snively and told her to send Norma Jean over. She came up and I stood next to her, about a foot or so away. She was wearing a tight, sleeveless sweater, so you could see the top of her bra under her arms. Her bra was filthy. As I stood next to her,

JEAN
SEX FOR
MERA. THE
UR WAIT
RTH IT.

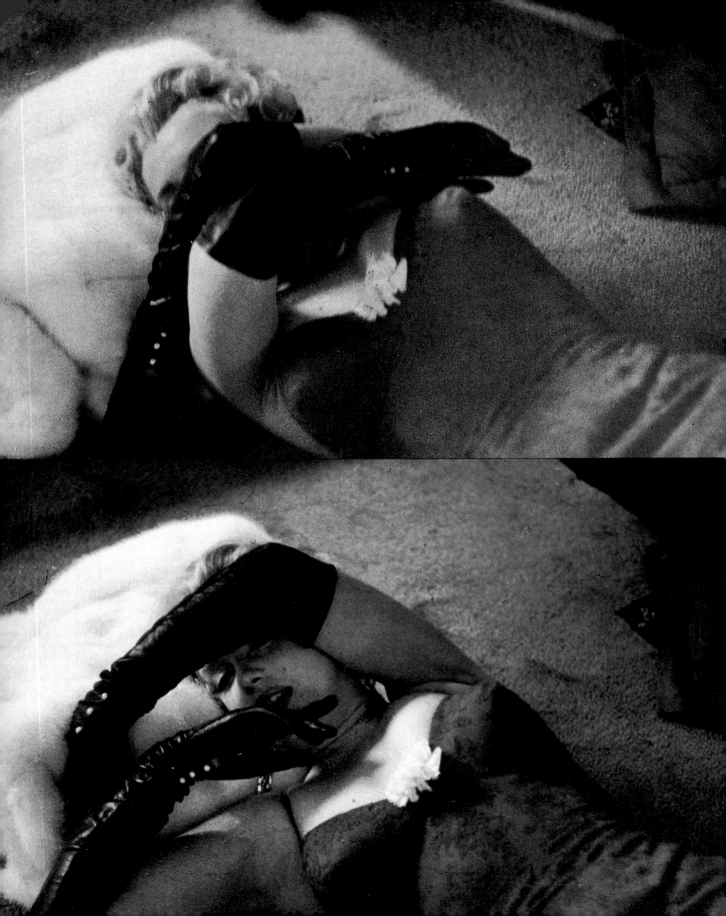

she smelled like she had not bathed. I thought to myself, "I can't introduce this girl to executives of Clairol." So I never used her until years later.

Then I told Norma Jean, "They want blond hair, and maybe it should be piled on top of your head." I took her hair and bunched it on top of her head, and it revealed that her neck was dirty. It must have been unwashed for a week.

I told Snively, because I couldn't tell it to the girl, "You better tell Norma Jean to take a bath, and to put on clean underwear. And to wear cologne, or use some antiperspirant."

By the time she signed her first contract at 20th Century-Fox she was a different person. When she became Marilyn Monroe, she was not the person that I knew as Norma Jean Dougherty. She was as though reborn into a new body, a new look, new hair. She was clean as a whistle as far as I could tell. I did not work with her too much, but the amount of time I did work with her, I could see that it was not the same girl who had hung around my office ten years earlier.

The *Saturday Evening Post* decided that since everybody else had done so much about Marilyn Monroe, the *Post* should do a centerfold on her. No life story or anything, just a centerfold and a little commentary about her. They asked me to shoot it.

I went out to her home, which was then in Beverly Glen in the far end of Beverly Hills, next to Bel Air. She was living with *Life* photographer Milton Greene and his wife. Greene met her when she was studying in New York and he did a picture story on her for *Life*. He and Marilyn got along very well.

The *Saturday Evening Post* was a very sedate magazine, and more a literary magazine than a photographic one. They said that they could not go to extremes, like *Playboy* or any of the other men's magazines. The most that they could do was to show cleavage on Marilyn and show her in a form-fitting dress.

She put on a bright red, lacy-type gown, very low cut. It was so low cut that we even put a flower in her bosom so the cleavage would not show much.

I was due there at about noon, and Marilyn was not supposed to have a lot of time to spend on this thing. I got there and spread out my equipment, and I waited and waited and nothing happened. I was told Marilyn was upstairs, but not quite ready. She kept me waiting six hours. It was a little after six o'clock when she finally came downstairs. What she was doing all day long, I have no idea. She evidently was upstairs that whole time. But she came down, and she sat on the stairs, and I went and sat beside her and she asked me where I wanted her.

"Right there, on the floor," I suggested, pointing to a spot in the living room in front of the fireplace. "I'm sure you've been on the floor before," I added with a smirk. She laughed.

Milton Greene, who had waited with me for the whole six hours, offered us a white fox furpiece to use as a pillow for her. Marilyn, wearing the tight, low-cut evening gown, took the direction, flopped on the floor, and as a starter, began to writhe. This was a very sexy scene, and watching her pose on the floor gave me some wild ideas.

Grabbing my 35mm Leica, which I always carried as a backup, I started to shoot fast action, one right after the other. "Keep it up!" I shouted. "Get wilder! Make believe you're going through the throes of ecstasy!" She continued her antics, flailing her arms over her head, then across her face, and uttering moans for sound effects. This was really wild and I kept firing away. This happened at least thirty years before the movie *When Harry Met Sally*, in which actress Meg Ryan shows Billy Crystal how she could really fake an orgasm. I wonder if they were copying my long-ago idea?

Chapter Eleven

I was friendly with a publicity man in New York named George Lottman, who in the early days handled quite a few radio people, including Bing Crosby. He knew I was going to the Coast so he said, "When you get out there, drop in and see Bing and give him my regards, will you? But I do want to warn you about one thing. With your camera, Bing is going be afraid of you. Don't try to take any pictures of him without his hat on or when he's not wearing his toupée."

I said, "Well, that's interesting. I'll see what happens when I meet him."

Once I was established in Hollywood I received a call from whoever was handling Bing's publicity, that I could come and shoot him during a dress rehearsal, not during earlier rehearsal because he wouldn't be in makeup "if you know what I mean." That is the way he put it.

I said, "You mean he won't be wearing his toupée? Might not even have his hat on or anything?"

I packed my camera gear in a big case. At the studio where the program originated, I was holding the camera in readiness, and Bing was standing at the microphone without a hat on and his head showing his baldness halfway back. He looked at me and he waved his hand, saying, "No pictures, no pictures."

I held my hand up to him and I said, "Bing, I'm all prepared for that." And I reached into my camera case.

I had taken some fur from a rug, and cut it up and pasted it onto a flashbulb like hair on a man's head, with a part in the middle, and I held it up to Bing, and I said, "See, I bring flashbulbs with hair on them."

Bing studied the bulb and started laughing. Then he said, "Do whatever the hell you want to do." He no longer cared, because I had pulled a fast one on him that he was

ERFORMING
RADIO
HERE, HIS
IS LONGTIME
BOB HOPE.

not prepared for. Bing never forgot that. From then on, he never ever worried about wearing his toupée or not, or wearing a hat when I was shooting his picture.

I used to cover every recording session Bing did when he was making records for Decca. He would stand in front of the mike and do his *bu-bu-bu-bu's*, and get away from some of the lyrics, and even harmonize some of the melody, rather than sing the melody itself. Jack Kapp, the owner of Decca Records, had a picture of Pocahontas, or some other Indian woman, looking up to the sky with arms raised and a very pleading look on her face, and they wrote a big caption under it: "Where's the melody?" As if she were saying, "Why are these guys singing and going all around the melody, when all Jack Kapp wanted was the melody."

One September, Bing was making a record for Christmas of "Ave Maria." There are two "Ave Marias," Schubert's and Gounod's, and Bing liked the melody of Schubert's, a little more melodic than Gounod's. Bing came to the recording session really drunk. It was pathetic. He stood up wobbling in front of the microphone and his voice quavered.

Jack Kapp said, "Bing, why don't you go and sit down. We'll give you some coffee. Relax, then we'll try to pick it up in half an hour or so." So Bing sat at the side of the room in a stupor, with his head at an angle. He was out of it. His legs were apart, and as I looked at him, I saw that there was a great big hole in his pants right in his crotch.

I walked over and I said, "Bing, do you realize you got a great big hole in your crotch, right there?" So he looks down, and he puts his finger in it and he said, "Oh, Jesus, hey, but that makes it convenient, doesn't it?"

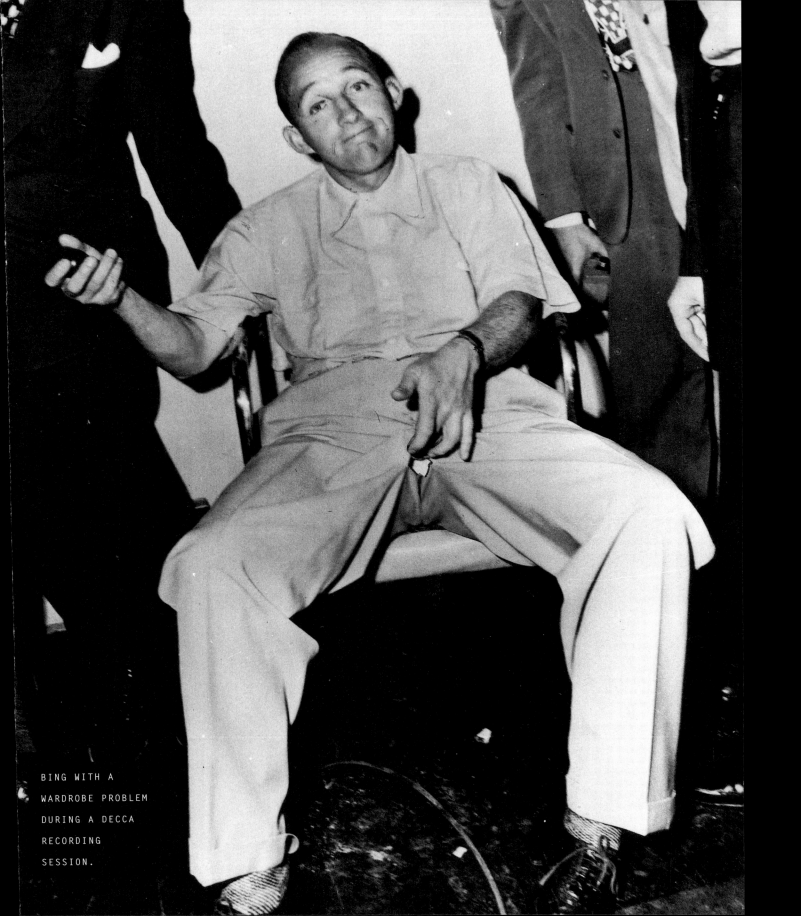

BING WITH A
WARDROBE PROBLEM
DURING A DECCA
RECORDING
SESSION.

Chapter Twelve

Wally Westmore at Paramount taught me how the studios made girls look busty for the screen, to give them a deeper cleavage. He mentioned how Paulette Goddard was very small busted, and he started explaining to me how they changed her look. She was in the makeup room with us at the time, so he demonstrated on her exactly how they took her boobs and taped them close together, just taped them with regular gaffer's tape, the same kind they used to tape things on the walls and tape up film cans and such. Paulette had no objection to this demonstration.

By taping boobs together, they had to add cotton on the sides. Then they put a wired bra on the girl. Usually they moved the straps on the bra from the center of the cup to the side of the cup, so that when the straps went over the shoulder, they were pulling in toward the middle, too.

It was through Paulette Goddard when she was married to Charlie Chaplin that I got to know Charlie pretty well. That was prior to his being asked to leave the country, I think he was shoved, not asked. He became a millionaire here but he never became a citizen of the United States. I do not think Charlie really had Communist leanings. I think Charlie was a guy who looked for equality in people.

Charlie used to sit in Ciro's nightclub and talk while I would get a picture of him with Paulette Goddard and then he would say, "Why don't you sit down? Can I buy you a drink?" I do not drink and I never smoked. I drank ginger ale only. I was probably the only Mr. Do-Nothing in Hollywood, because every other photographer would sit there with booze. But maybe that is one reason why so many stars respected me and were able to open up with me.

ETTE GODDARD
WILLIAM
LL ON
O'S *SCREEN*
D *PLAYHOUSE*.

Charlie used to tell me a lot of stories about himself. For me that was fascinating, because as a kid, this guy was my idol. I felt that Charlie Chaplin was really the guy who made the movie industry.

Not too long ago, on a visit to London while filming a documentary, I stepped into a Kosher deli just off Carnaby Street. Seated at a rear table, I was studying the menu when the eighty-five-year-old owner stopped by and spied my Bolex movie camera lying on the chair beside me. "You're an American, aren't you?" he asked. When I nodded in reply, he said that I was sitting at Charlie Chaplin's table. Then he told me how, when he was a little boy and his father ran the deli (Bloom's was the name), he would sit and schmooze with Chaplin.

CHARLIE CHAPLIN AND PAULETTE GODDARD AT
CIRO'S NIGHTCLUB.

Chapter Thirteen

Hedda Hopper was a former actress who became a Hollywood columnist when her acting career started to wane. Hedda was a two-fisted newspaperwoman. She swore like a trooper; she pulled no punches. If she wanted to know something, if she wanted to know if a guy was sleeping with somebody, she would turn right around to him and demand, "Who are you sleeping with? Are you really shacking up with so and so?"

Such direct questioning would take these people aback and they would either blurt out the truth, or else they would shy away from her. Hedda really was what we called a newspaper broad.

Hedda got herself a gossip show on radio where she would sit at the microphone, as if she were a female Walter Winchell. I was assigned to cover her radio show and found she had one little fetish: she loved hats and always wore kooky, crazy hats. She would take them to the broadcast and then sit at a microphone and wear one hat during the early part of the broadcast. In the middle of the show she would then figure she needed a change; sometimes she would wear three and four hats during a broadcast. They were always wild hats.

She was a very likable woman, and you did not need to watch your etiquette speaking to her, or call her Miss Hopper. You just called her Hedda.

Hedda had a home in Beverly Hills, in the Beverly Drive section north of Sunset Boulevard, where a lot of show people and the rich and famous all lived, a beautiful Spanish-style home where she used to throw big parties. I was assigned to cover many of them. I got a lot of shots of scenes like George Sanders standing up singing while José Iturbi was playing the piano for him.

Hedda Hopper fell into two categories, being both a member of the press and an actress, so she understood what had to be done to make her parties effective vehicles

A WOULD
N CHANGE
  DURING HER
EEN-MINUTE
IP PROGRAM.

for publicity. She knew how to make this stuff newsworthy. If, at a dinner, everybody was just sitting around and doing nothing, that party was not worth publicizing. But if somebody got up and made a toast to somebody else and then they all threw their glasses into the fireplace, that was a story that a publicist could place in a newspaper or magazine.

Her son, Bill Hopper, was not only an actor (on the original "Perry Mason" TV series) but also a car salesman who worked at the Hollywood Cadillac agency just across the street from my Vine Street studio. Every day he would drop by and dish some Hollywood dirt he'd learned from his mother.

He was well over six feet tall, and when I stood next to him we were like Mutt and Jeff. I am only five feet, five and a half inches. But over the years I did manage to buy three Cadillacs from him.

COMEDIAN KEN MURRAY JUDGING
A HAT CONTEST BETWEEN CARMEN MIRANDA
AND HEDDA HOPPER.

AT A PARTY AT
HEDDA HOPPER'S
BEVERLY HILLS
HOME, ACTOR
GEORGE SANDERS
SINGS WHILE
JOSÉ ITURBI
HANDLES THE
PIANO DUTIES.

IN CIRO'S NIGHTCLUB, OWNER HERMAN HOVER
INTERRUPTS A DATE BETWEEN HEDDA HOPPER
AND ACTOR MARK STEVENS TO WHISPER
A BIT OF GOSSIP INTO THE COLUMNIST'S EAR.

HEDDA AND ONE OF HER
FAMOUS HATS.

Chapter Fourteen

When Julie Andrews was making the film *Mary Poppins*, the only time she could give me to shoot publicity stills was New Year's Day. Tom Jones, the publicist at Disney, worried about the shoot, telling me, "She may have gone out to a party the night before, and she may not look good. But you're going to have to do the best you can." New Year's morning about ten o'clock or so, I opened up my studio and made sure the dressing room was clean.

Julie walked in. She had brought some wardrobe with her, and hung it in the dressing room. I stood there looking at her, and I finally sat her down and said, "Julie, I can't photograph you the way you look now." She looked at me startled, like what did she get up for on New Year's Day? Why had she come to my studio if we were not going to work?

"Your face is long," I told her. "You have a long distance from your hair line to your chin line. That bothers me." I asked her if she minded if I tried to make her more photogenic and she gave me carte blanche.

"I've got to shorten your forehead." I started with her hair. "Let's take some of your hair and comb it down to bangs, just a little above your eyebrows." She stood in front of this full-length mirror and she got her bangs down to her eyebrows. "Now I want to shorten your chin," I told her, "but we can't do any surgery here, so we're going to have to hide it with either lighting, or by you resting your chin on your arms while you're leaning on the back of a chair."

As we were going along, I kept seeing a look on Julie I realized that she had never even known she had. It turned out that she had always been bothered by the fact that her face was long. But she had a lovely face, and whenever she talked, it was like sparkles coming out of her mouth. And the voice of this girl absolutely enthralled me.

IE ANDREWS
SCAR NIGHT.
IE'S NEW
STYLE—FOR
FIRST TIME.

About halfway through this sitting, she was standing up. I went over and I put my arms on her shoulder. We were almost nose to nose, and I said, "Julie, you look lovely. I would leave my wife for you," and she started laughing and I paused, "two or three nights a week." She howled with laughter. That put her in a completely different mood and we made some great pictures. But she absolutely had an image you could fall in love with.

That was my way of shooting women. I had to see a love image in a woman before I could photograph her. I once told *Look* magazine that in the years that I photographed Hollywood stars and starlets, and even ordinary people, I had fallen in love with over three thousand women. Casanova has nothing on me. Julie topped the list.

Julie loved that look. Whenever I would bump into her after that she would look at me and point to her hair. She wore that hairdo until she made the movie *Victor/Victoria*, which was nearly twenty years later.

JULIE ANDREWS AT HOME WITH
DAUGHTER EMMA KATE
JUST AFTER *MARY POPPINS* WAS SHOT
AND BEFORE WORK STARTED ON
THE SOUND OF MUSIC.

OSCAR NIGHT
WITH TONY
WALTON,
JULIE'S FIRST
HUSBAND.

JULIE'S NEW
HAIRSTYLE.

Chapter Fifteen

Dick Van Dyke was sent to me shortly after Julie. Dick had gone from *Mary Poppins* to a film called *Lt. Robin Crusoe, USN*. Dick came in and right away we hit it off; we were telling each other jokes, both keeling over with laughter.

When Stan Laurel was very sick, Charlton Heston, Dana Andrews, and I drove out to Laurel's apartment at the beach, to present him with a Screen Actors Guild Award. I had known Stan in the past, with Ollie Hardy, so this was kind of a renewed acquaintance with him. After he received the award, I told Stan I would send him a couple of prints. A few days later I called him up and told him I had some pictures ready and I wanted to come out and drop them off and spend some time with him. Being very ill, he wanted company. Not too many people were coming to visit him at that time.

Dick Van Dyke was in the office when I called. He asked, "Is that Stan Laurel?"

"Yeah," I told him. "I'm going out to see him tonight"

"Can I go with you?" Dick wanted to know. Stan was still on the phone, so I asked him if he minded if I brought Dick Van Dyke along.

Stan says, "Oh my God, yes. He does me very well."

That evening we brought the prints to Stan. I went out to visit, but I became the observer. Luckily I brought my camera. Dick and Stan were doing things that were hilarious. Dick would get up and do some funny schtick as if he were playing a Laurel character, scratching his head and making the distinct Stan Laurel faces.

Stan would say, "No, you do it like this," and he would take Dick's face and he'd start molding it, and I kept on snapping pictures.

This turned out to be the funniest and most rewarding evening I ever spent. Stan had been in the doldrums for several days and this visit with Dick Van Dyke gave

him the life that he needed. To me it was so delightfully funny that I could have stayed all night watching Stan teaching Dick how to be Stan Laurel.

It was unfortunate that within a few months Stan died. Dick and I attended the funeral service, and Dick delivered the eulogy. When the service was over I remarked that it was shameful that no other comedians had attended aside from Buster Keaton. "Let's get even with them," I suggested. "Let's do a television special . . . 'A Salute to Stan Laurel' . . . and make all those other comics who stole material from Stan and Ollie appear on it."

As a result, I put together the show as a one-hour special and sold it to Doyle-Dane-Bernbach agency for Monsanto Chemical. Buster Keaton, Lucille Ball, Bob Newhart, Danny Kaye—all appeared on the show gratis, with Dick Van Dyke hosting and doing his Stan Laurel impersonation.

STAN LAUREL
TEACHES DICK
VAN DYKE TO
IMPERSONATE
STAN PROPERLY.

AT WORK WITH
DICK.

WHEN THE
HOLLYWOOD
VICTORY
CARAVAN WENT
ON A BOND-
SELLING TOUR
DURING WORLD
WAR II,
LAUREL AND
HARDY FOOLED
AROUND WITH
STARLET ALMA
CARROLL.

STAN AT WORK

WITH PARTNER

OLIVER HARDY.

LAUREL AND HARDY
WITH STARLETS ON THE VICTORY
CARAVAN BOND-SELLING TOUR.

Chapter Sixteen

I got to know Alfred Hitchcock when the *Saturday Evening Post* sent me out to shoot him while he was making the movie *Lifeboat*. I found him not to be the mysterious man of his reputation; Hitchcock was a totally different guy.

He used to work for an advertising agency. He had no embarrassment about his weight, no embarrassment about how he would look in a photograph. He was a funny guy. He liked to pull jokes on people. Every time he saw me get ready to take a shot, he would turn on a strange face. He would not be Alfred Hitchcock. He would scratch his head, pick his nose, or do some crazy thing so I never could get just a good, honest-looking face of Hitchcock.

This went on, exposure after exposure after exposure. The minute I would pick up the camera, he put a pencil up his nose, or he was biting on something, or he was making a strange face. I used every device I knew to make him unaware that I was shooting. I put the longest telephoto lens on that I had, a 250mm, and went to the far end of the studio, trying to shoot him when he was preoccupied by other work. But he seemed to know all my tricks. I was trying to fool him, and he was trying to fool me. It was a game. I finally got a lot of pictures of Alfred Hitchcock, but instead of taking maybe thirty or forty pictures, which you'd usually do in a session like that, I took three hundred or four hundred. He was a film waster, but I found him to be delightful. I never brought up the fact that he was lousing me up; he never brought up the fact that he was trying to do something to me. It was just an unspoken game between us.

His movies bring out the ominous and mysterious side of man. I wanted to get a little bit of that ominous thing about Alfred Hitchcock in my pictures. That is why I took his silhouette, which to me is a classic. Here is a big hulk of a man, you do not see his face. You do not see anything at all except a black, black blotch against a light

D HITCHCOCK
S MADE FACES
HE SUSPECTED
AMERA WAS
M.

background and you cannot help but recognize this hulk. There is no other man who would look like that in a silhouette. A big blob just sitting in a director's chair. Who else could it be but Hitchcock?

HITCH STRIKES
A FAMILIAR POSE.

PERHAPS HIS MOST FAMOUS

POSE OF ALL.

Chapter Seventeen

Charlton Heston and I became really good friends as a result of my taking pictures of him on *The Ten Commandments*. When I was asked by the *Saturday Evening Post* to do the illustrations for Heston's life story, it was an easy matter, because by then I knew him and had worked with him before.

Chuck told me at one time that when he and his wife, Lydia, were in New York during the early days of their marriage, he worked as a nude male model for art classes. He had a tremendous physique, a big guy with a big chest, very muscular.

I said, "We should show your physique for the *Post* story."

"I'll tell you what," said Heston, "You can take photographs of me in my steambath." He got stripped down, totally nude, and then got into the steambath. There I was photographing Chuck Heston in the nude. I made him put a towel across his middle so at least we would not to show everything.

Heston was president of the Screen Actors Guild (SAG) for several terms. He would throw parties at his house after Guild meetings and SAG would ask me to go to take whatever candid photos I could of all the delegates so they could run them in their magazine. One night, my Hasselblad jammed. What to do? What to do? Chuck's wife Lydia, a lovely, very attractive woman, also had a Hasselblad just like mine.

In front of the whole crowd, I turned to Chuck and asked, "Do you mind if I use your wife's equipment tonight?" Overhearing this, the crowd started roaring. I thought to myself: "What did I say?" All I wanted to do was borrow her Hasselblad. Then it dawned on me that here I was standing between him and her, and she was wearing a very lovely dress which showed her off beautifully, and I was looking at her. But Lydia saved the evening for me by loudly announcing, "Sure, Gene, you can use my camera!"

LE ASKED ME
KE STILLS
STON'S
   IN *THE TEN*
NDMENTS.

Chuck and Lydia have been very kind to me. When I wrote an article about Lydia's work for a photo magazine, both of them gladly spent an afternoon posing for a color cover. Another time, NASA sent me three cameras that had been to the moon and back to be used in a documentary film I was producing. Chuck and Lydia came to our camera club meeting and unveiled the NASA equipment for the members to inspect.

Still later, when Gene Ostroff, the curator of photography for the Smithsonian Institution, came the the West Coast on a lecture tour, I, as president of the American Society of Camera Collectors, and my wife, Gloria, were to host a formal dinner party for him. I asked the Hestons to cohost the affair, and they agreed enthusiastically. As a result Chuck and I presented Ostroff with one of my photos of Heston as Moses. It now hangs in the Smithsonian.

CHUCK ON THE TENNIS COURT WITH
EFREM ZIMBALIST, JR.

114

CHUCK AND I
DISCUSS HIS
CAMERA TECHNIQUE.

Chapter Eighteen

I knew Ronald Reagan many years before he became President. I joined a Warner Brothers junket up to Reno for the premiere of *Virginia City*. It was an Errol Flynn picture, and Ronnie was along on that trip.

Warners staged a parade down Virginia Street under the arch that says, "Reno, the Biggest Little City in the World." Every photographer was given a convertible car and a driver by the Reno Chamber of Commerce, to provide them the position they wanted in the parade, to follow it, to zigzag in and out of it, to get their photographs.

Ronald Reagan was never, ever considered an important person when I was taking pictures. For that parade, we always shoved him into the back when we arranged the actors. I still have one of those photographs with all the important people in the foreground, and if you look closely at the left side of the line-up, you can recognize Ronald Reagan.

That particular occasion, I was riding in my convertible myself and I noticed that William Holden was standing around and nobody had provided him with a horse to ride in the parade. Bill was one of the most promising up-and-coming actors of the time. He was not a top star yet. *Sunset Boulevard* and *Stalag 17* and *Bridge on the River Kwai* were years away. But Bill was making consistently good pictures, and he was standing there looking lost.

We did not know him as William Holden; we knew him as Billy Beedle — that was his real name.

"Billy, where's your horse?" I called out to him. He looked at me and shrugged his shoulders.

I said, "Why don't you come on in the car with me?"

"Yeah, but I'm supposed to be in the parade," he said.

"The hell with that, I'll give you a Speed Graphic," I yelled, and I gave him my Speed Graphic and told him, "you shoot some pictures with me." I took out the backup Leica for myself.

He climbed into my car and we rode through the parade, Bill Holden shooting along side of me. I had the most expensive assistant that anybody could possible have, working for me, and nobody even knew who he was, because he was standing around with a camera. You take a guy like that and you put him out of context, nobody will pay any attention to him.

RONALD REAGAN IS ON HORSE
TO RIGHT OF THE FLAG
BEARER IN THIS GROUP PHOTO
TAKEN IN RENO, NEVADA.

Chapter Nineteen

When Lana Turner first appeared on the screen as a sixteen- or eighteen-year-old girl in a Mervyn LeRoy movie called *They Won't Forget*, she was shown walking down the street in a tight sweater. That was as much as they showed of Lana Turner: a pretty young girl with a beautiful body in a very tight sweater. It caused a sensation.

She was sexier in that scene to the viewing audience than Madonna is in *Truth or Dare* when she opens up her blouse and bares her breasts. It was done tastefully in the Lana Turner movie; it was done blatantly in the Madonna thing. The imagination in the audience's mind built a better picture than the reality that Madonna showed. And Madonna's boobs aren't that attractive.

Years after coming to Hollywood, I met this girl who was perhaps twenty at the time, under contract to MGM, and just as pretty as I remembered her in *They Won't Forget*. I was asked to do a picture layout of her for a fan magazine. She lived in a little apartment on Sunset Plaza, just off Sunset Strip, and she invited me up to her place. She wore her trademark tight sweater, and it was quite a thrill for me to spend the time with her.

After that first photo session, I saw Lana at quite a few of the parties we Hollywood photographers used to cover. At one in particular, a garden party by a swimming pool, Lana was there in a beautiful little play suit and looked as sexy as anything imaginable. I and the other photographers were asked if we wanted to jump into our swim suits and join the group in the pool.

After I changed into bathing trunks, Lana came over and started talking to me. I started beating my chest saying, "Me Tarzan, you Jane." Right near me was a fig tree, right near the pool. I took one of those big fig leaves off the tree and I attached it to the front of my bathing suit and ran over and grabbed Lana, and yelled, "Me Adam, you

Eve." I grabbed her in my arms and I bent her over, as though I was really going to devour her.

Moments like that provided one of the special fringe benefits of my job. In what other business can a little schnook from a small Massachusetts town get to hobnob with glamorous movie queens and be accepted as one of the crowd?

That's why Hollywood was fun in those days.

LANA BECAME A STAR AS A RESULT
OF A THIRTY-SECOND BIT IN A TIGHT
SWEATER IN *THEY WON'T FORGET*. HERE,
SHE STRUTS HER STUFF.

LANA EATS
CORN AT
A POOL PARTY—
NOT YOUR
TYPICAL STUDIO
PUBLICITY SHOT.

Chapter Twenty

Once I did a story in the *Saturday Evening Post* about the crazy hairdos that the kids were wearing — the ducktail and the Mohawk. This was not quite as ridiculous as today's spiked hair, but was pretty crazy. During my work on this assignment, I got a call from the Paramount studios publicity department announcing that they had just signed a girl from New York who had the craziest hairdo anybody would want to see. It was Shirley MacLaine.

I came down to the studio and I met this young girl. They had borrowed Jerry Lewis's dressing room so that we could have a place to take pictures, an appropriate atmosphere to show her combing her hair. Jerry and Dean Martin were making a movie at the time. It was an inside dressing room, not a little bungalow outside. Jerry kept coming over to watch what was going on because he himself was a photography nut.

Somebody suggested that Shirley might comb her hair with an eggbeater — which is an old gag. You see a guy with messy hair, you say, "What did you do, comb your hair with an eggbeater?"

"Hey, let's get an eggbeater," I agreed. The prop man on any set keeps what they call a prop box, and you can name almost anything that you want and the prop man can reach into his box and get it. Jerry Lewis came back from the prop box with an eggbeater. I took pictures of Shirley combing her hair with the eggbeater. We were shooting the pictures, I make two or three negatives, and Jerry said, "Hey, let me borrow your camera, I'd like to take some too." Jerry took my Rolleiflex and he started fiddling around with it, focusing it, playing with the shutter, and the camera jammed. Luckily, I had already gotten my pictures. I wound the film up and got the roll out, and Jerry said, "Look, I'm going to fix this camera." He took it from me and went back on the set where the whole movie company was waiting for him to start doing some more

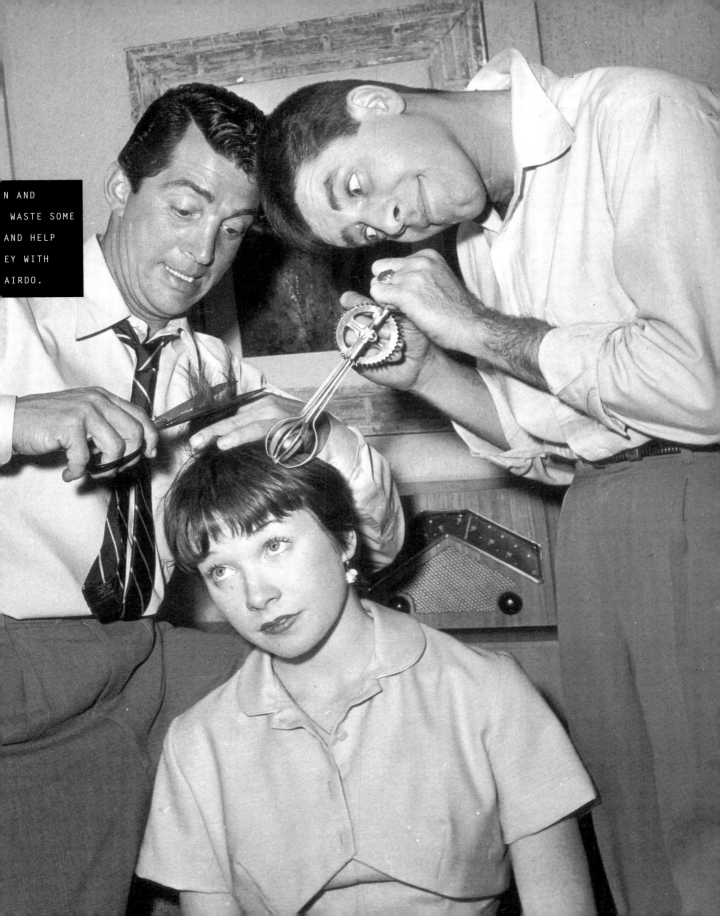

scenes. Jerry called the grip, who had all the tools, and he made himself a table on the set. He sat down and decided, the hell with the movie, he was going to fix my camera.

That is exactly what he did. He spent almost an hour working on the damn camera. I waited there, thinking that the director and the producer are going to murder me, they are never going to allow me on their sets again, because it is costing them a fortune for Jerry to be doing this. It turned out that some little thing had disconnected in the mechanism, and Jerry finally caught it, and the camera was working again.

In those days, when most movies were in black and white, it cost about $20,000 an hour to make a film. Jerry spent about three quarters of an hour working on my camera, so I figure the repair job cost Paramount $15,000. That was probably the most expensive repair job ever done on a camera.

SHIRLEY COMBS HER HAIR
WITH AN EGGBEATER.

MARTIN AND LEWIS.

WHILE REHEARSING FOR THE "COLGATE COMEDY
HOUR," JERRY BET ME A MILLION
DOLLARS THAT I COULD NOT GET BOTH THE
STAGE ACTION AND THE TV MONITOR IN THE SAME
SHOT. HE NEVER PAID UP.

Chapter Twenty-One

When I was living in back of my studio on the Sunset Strip, Cary Grant used to come over several evenings a week while he was working at RKO and Columbia. I stored copies of his and other stars' movies at my office, and they would lend each other prints for home showings. I would take care of the films and rewind them and see that there were no breaks in them and that all the perforations were good.

Cary lived at the beach, so he used to go down Sunset Boulevard and stop at my place on his way home to pick up a film for the evening. We would sit around and talk. Sometimes he would say, "Hey, why don't we go out and have dinner together." At that time I was single, and he was single. He was going out with Barbara Hutton, but I did not know he was running around with her. He kept it kind of quiet; there was not much publicity about his courtship. She was the richest woman in the world at that time.

Cary liked kosher food, so we used to go up to the Hollywood Roosevelt Hotel where there was a Jewish deli. We would eat matzo ball and kreplach soup and stuff like that for dinner, and then he would drop me at my studio and continue on to the beach.

One evening, I got a phone call from Cary Grant, and he asked me what I was doing the next day.

"Why don't you call [your wife] Gloria," he said, "and ask her if she'd like to come with you up to Lake Arrowhead tomorrow morning and meet me there around eleven o'clock?"

"What's going on up at Lake Arrowhead?" I asked him.

"Oh, nothing," he told me. "I just thought maybe you'd like to come on up and bring your camera up there. It's very picturesque. You'll be able to take some nice pictures. So come on up there and meet with me."

He had method in his madness but I did not know what was going on. However

I called Gloria and let her know that Cary Grant had invited us to drive up to Lake Arrowhead. We had just had a major argument and she said she was still angry with me and declined the offer. I had no interest in driving all the way up there all alone, so I called Cary back and told him we couldn't make it.

"I'd love to have you come up with me," he sounded a little disappointed, "but if that's the case, okay."

That evening, the Los Angeles newspapers came out with big headlines: CARY GRANT MARRIES BARBARA HUTTON AT LAKE ARROWHEAD. Now, either he wanted me to come up there and just attend, or he wanted me to come up there and take pictures for him. There were no pictures of the wedding that I ever saw.

I wish he had told me what his plans were. I would have kept his secret and certainly would have driven up all alone just to have an exclusive on a story like that. But that was the way Cary acted. He was secretive about his private life and when we were together, I never tried to ferret out what his intentions or what his ideas were.

When he showed his 16mm movies at his beach place, he used to project them on the wall; he did not have a screen. I had a big screen and he used to borrow it from my studio or home and the next evening return it. Why he never bought a movie screen, I cannot imagine.

When Cary Grant would drive up my street and the neighbors would be out watering the lawn or something they would come to me later and say, "Hey, was that Cary Grant I saw pull up in front of your house?" Here we are in a little middle-class section of the Valley, and all of a sudden, here was Cary Grant, one of the biggest stars of the movies, hanging around our neighborhood. It caused quite a little talk around there.

Later, after he married Barbara Hutton, I wondered, what could I give Cary Grant and Barbara for a wedding present? A guy married to the richest woman in the world. They had everything; she owned all the five and tens. I decided to give them a movie screen.

It was fun in those days when movies were mainly in the major theaters, picture palaces they were, and there we were showing these same movies in our homes but on a small screen and with a home machine. It was a novelty. Of course, today you see all these movies on videotape, and it is not anything special to show a movie at home.

While the producers had professional type screening rooms in their homes, I had a 16mm projector in my studio and would run movie parties every Sunday night for

RISE STEVENS, METROPOLITAN OPERA STAR,
KIBITZES CARY GRANT'S GIN RUMMY GAME ABOARD
THE VICTORY CARAVAN TRAIN.

the young Hollywood crowd. Bob Stack, Jackie Cooper, Laraine Day, Bonita Granville, and many lesser known players would be constant visitors. Mine was the "in" place on Sundays. Hedda Hopper and Louella Parsons regularly mentioned my parties in their gossip columns.

BACKSTAGE DURING ONE
OF THE VICTORY CARAVAN
PERFORMANCES. CARY,
BING CROSBY, AND PAT O'BRIEN.

Chapter Twenty-Two

O f the many movie stars with whom I have had dealings, Lou Costello became the closest friend. I had met him originally in New York when I was working with the radio version of the "Kate Smith Show" on CBS. One night Abbott and Costello were guest stars on the program, and I discovered that Costello was interested in photography.

Years later, after they were well established, Lou and I traveled back to New York together. We bumped into two girls in the hotel elevator. They went ga-ga over Lou. They recognized him immediately, and they said, "Oh, gee, Mr. Costello, and blah, blah, blah, blah." Lou invited them up to our suite. The next morning when I woke up, Lou was still in bed. I had breakfast sent up.

When he came out of his bedroom, he said, "Gene, did I give you any money yesterday, or lend you any money?"

"No, Lou," I told him, "I never asked you for any money."

"But I had two thousand dollars in my pants pocket when I went to sleep," he was upset. "And it's gone."

"When did those girls leave?" I asked.

"I don't know," he said. "I was falling asleep and I don't remember." He was more than a little bit drunk, too, at the end of the evening and now two thousand bucks was missing. To me, at that time, it was like a million bucks.

That evening when we came back to the hotel after dinner, there was a note in our mailbox. Lou opened it and there were eighteen hundred dollars in the envelope and a note from one of the girls saying, "Dear Mr. Costello: I took the money last night when you were dozing off and my conscience hurt so badly that I just couldn't hold on to it. But I needed money for rent. I was so desperate to find money for rent, that's why

I took it. I didn't know that you had that much money, so I took out the money to pay my rent, and someday I will pay you back the rest of it."

After we got back from New York, a month went by and Lou called me up.

"Gene, you'll never guess what happened," he said. "You know those two broads that came up to our hotel room at the Warwick that night and took the money? They're out here in Hollywood and the girl called me up and she brought me the rest of the money. So you know what I did? I'm a good-hearted guy. I took the broads over to Universal and got them each a screen test."

During my army days at Fort MacArthur, I would borrow films from Lou's collection to show to the troops down at the base in San Pedro. One day I called Lou's house to ask if I could come out and pick up a film.

The maid answered and her voice was down. "Yes," she said about my picking up the movie, "but there's trouble here." She refused to tell me what was wrong over the phone. When I got to Lou's house, there was an ambulance out front. The medics were working on his little one-year-old son, Lou Jr. He had fallen in the swimming pool and drowned.

Lou was not even home. He was at NBC. He and Bud had a radio show there and they were at the rehearsal. Despite the fact that his baby drowned that afternoon, Lou and Bud did their radio show that night. It would have been too late to put in an alternate show or replay an old one because in those days they did not have the recording systems they have today. They used to put the shows on big sixteen-inch platters and the quality when you played them was poor.

The two of them went on the air and Lou made the announcement before the show started, "You talk about show business," he told the audience, "and the fact that the show must go on. My baby just died this afternoon and I have to go on the air and be funny."

And he and Bud performed that dreadful night.

ABBOTT AND COSTELLO
WITH VOCALIST
CONNIE HAINES ON
THEIR 1942
RADIO PROGRAM.

THE RARELY
PHOTOGRAPHED
VOICE OF BUGS
BUNNY AND HIS
PALS, MEL BLANC,
WITH BUD AND
LOU IN MY
STUDIO. *TOP*
THE ANDREWS
SISTERS WITH BUD
AND LOU. *BOTTOM*

CONNIE HAINES
AND LOU AT
THE COSTELLO
HOME. *TOP*
BUD AND LOU IN
ONE OF THEIR
STANDARD
ROUTINES. *BOTTOM*

Chapter Twenty-Three

My old roommate, Marty Melcher, was married first to Patti Andrews (of the Andrews Sisters) and then dumped her for Doris Day, when Doris was an up-and-coming star and the Andrews Sisters were starting to fade from the spotlight. When Patti finally found out that Marty was leaving her for Doris, the two of them had a fight that was unbelievable to watch, a real cat and dog fight.

One night, Fox threw a fancy party after having had a worldwide contest for Doris Day look-alikes. They brought about sixty or seventy girls from all over the world to Hollywood. I made a short movie of the Doris Day look-alikes and at the party they would pick the winner. Doris was to present her with the award.

Jim Denton, the publicity man at 20th Century-Fox, said to me, "Gene, you're going to have trouble." I was shooting the party for the short. "Doris doesn't like this kind of thing," he told me. "She may not even show up. But if she does I want you to have not just one camera rolling, I want you to have two or three cameras rolling, so that you're getting her from every which angle, because I don't think she's going to let you take more than two minutes of movies, if that. And then she'll throw you the hell out of there."

There was an orchestra there, and tables and a dance floor. It was a dinner for the press. The studio really did it up brown. Finally, Marty and Doris walked in, and he said, "Doris, here's the guy who brought me to California. I was his roommate for two years before we met. This is the guy responsible for my being here."

Doris ran over and gave me a hug saying, "Gene, I'm glad to see you." We were hugging and walking onto the soundstage at the same time. The bandleader spotted Doris and started the music from the picture they were promoting.

She grabbed me and we danced into the room to applause. For her, not me. I explained to her that I was making the publicity movie and needed all this on film. She agreed to do whatever my crew needed. Here we were hoping to get a minute or two of Doris Day, and we wound up that evening getting two and a half hours of film of Doris for the studio. The studio could not believe it and it was all because when she walked in, Marty made that introduction.

That is the way things happened in Hollywood. Just because I happened to know certain people, I got a lot of things done.

FRAME FROM A 16MM FILM
OF DORIS DAY JUDGING A
DORIS DAY LOOK-ALIKE
CONTEST.

Chapter Twenty-Four

One night at dinner in the house, I was telling my wife, Gloria, how I was going to film Rex Harrison, who had been signed to do the movie *Doctor Dolittle* at 20th Century-Fox. This was during the days when I was making documentary films.

My wife turned to me in the middle of the meal and she said to me, "Rex Harrison! Wow, is he handsome!"

I sat there and looked at her and I said, "He is like hell! Gloria, you are married to me and I am the handsome man in your life, not Rex Harrison."

"Well, I can't help it," she said, "I think he's a very handsome guy."

The next morning, I was out on the set, and everybody was telling me what a bad mood Harrison was in. From what I had learned during other days of shooting, Rex was really difficult to get along with. He was nasty to everybody; he had a problem with his stomach from some kind of a sickness he had had in his early days.

That morning, while he was getting dressed, I walked over to him and said, "Rex, I'm Gene Lester. I'm going to make a movie for publicity to run on television, showing how *Doctor Dolittle* is being filmed." I explained that it was a documentary on the making of the film which would appear on over a hundred television stations. He did not say a thing, did not even answer me. He just gave me a very glum look.

When I encountered this kind of resistance from stars, I would always try to find some sort of common denominator to break the tension and create a friendly working relationship. That morning I just continued talking at him after a long pause.

"Rex," I went on, "I've got to tell you something that happened last night, and I don't know how you're going to feel about it." And I told him the story of what occurred at dinner and how my wife had said that he is handsome and I had said, "He is like hell."

He started laughing. I think it was the first time I had ever seen Rex Harrison really laugh since I met him.

"Why don't we call the still man over here," Harrison said to me, "and have him take a picture of both of us, and you show it to your wife. You and I'll be standing side by side, and let her decide who is the more handsome man in her life."

The next afternoon, Rex came over to me and he said, "Now I remember where I have known you before. You're that little bastard who made me take off my pants when you did my life story pictures in the *Saturday Evening Post*."

"Yes, I am that little bastard," I acknowledged. We got along great after that. I had thought it would be very interesting to show this elegant Englishman without pants, being waited on hand and foot by his butler, standing there in his shirttails, dressing up for an evening out, while his butler held the legs of his trousers and Rex stepped into them, with his garters on his feet, and his shirttails hanging down — pantless.

OF ME AND REX HARRISON ON
THE *DOCTOR DOLITTLE* SET FOR MY WIFE
TO JUDGE WHO WAS MORE HANDSOME.

Chapter Twenty-Five

I was assigned to shoot publicity pictures of "The Edgar Bergen Radio Show With Charlie McCarthy and Mortimer Snerd" and I got to know Edgar very well during those days because each week I had to cover the show. I found out that Edger was a real die-hard photography buff. Edgar used to come by my office quite often, and we established a rapport as photographers, rather than as a star and a photographer.

Each week I still covered his radio show with the dummies. He forbid anybody — including me — ever to take pictures of him putting Charlie McCarthy in the suitcase in which he carried Charlie, because Charlie would no longer look like a human being. I honored that demand. I stayed away from Charlie in the suitcase at the studio, but one day, at his home, I snuck a picture of Charlie when Edgar had stepped out of the room, a picture of Charlie lying there in his case.

Once, Edgar asked if I would come up to his house and do some pictures for him, of him with the dummies. I have a whole series of shots of Edgar and Charlie — with Charlie as a cowboy, Charlie as a sailor, Charlie as a 007, and that sort of thing. That day after I was through with Charlie, Edgar brought out a little baby.

He sat this baby on his lap, just like Charlie had been sitting a few minutes before.

All I could say was, "Gee." I was amazed. Here I had come to do these pictures with Charlie, and the dummies, and now he was manipulating this little baby. It was Candice Bergen when she was a year old. He worked her for me like a dummy. She could not talk much, at a year old; she was just sitting on his lap, just the way the dummies had been. But he was making funny jokes with the baby rather than with Mortimer Snerd, or with Charlie McCarthy.

Chapter Twenty-Six

Among the recording artists at Decca Records — where I shot many publicity pictures — were singers like Bing Crosby, Al Jolson, and Fred Astaire. One evening, I was at the studio when Al Jolson was recording some of his typical hits, the ones that made him famous, like "Mammy," "California Here I Come," and "Swanee." Halfway into the session, Bing Crosby came in. Bing was going to do something on one of the tracks with Al Jolson. While they were sitting there talking over the thing, Al was telling Bing, "You've got to sing it like a Yiddish cantor would do it."

Bing was an Irishman, and it was difficult to imagine that Bing, who had that melodic baritone voice, was going to start singing like a Jewish cantor. But Jolson tried to teach him how. He took Bing's face, and he contorted it. He put his hand around his neck, and he said, "Now sing m'yeaahh, m'yeaaahh." Bing was trying, "M'yeaahh, m'yeaahh." It was funny to watch and hear because they were such direct opposites when it came to singing. I wish I had a recording of the event. It would have been historical and hysterical.

Fred Astaire was also at that session and Jolson tried to make Astaire sound like a cantor next. It was an evening of just plain fun. In other words, even when these stars were serious with their work, doing things like making records, they had plenty of fun while they did it. They did not do their work as strict business. They were doing their work and were having fun. And I, too, had fun making my photographs under those circumstances. It's a pity that there is no record of the shenanigans that took place at this session. I think a record of the rehearsal would have sold just as many copies as the masters they were aiming for. Actors and singers were not always perfect in their renditions and they made many bloopers. Those were just as much part of the entertainment business as the final released product.

AL JOLSON TRYING TO TEACH BING CROSBY
TO GET WHAT JOLIE CALLED
"THE JEWISH TEAR IN HIS VOICE"
AND MAKE THE IRISH CROONER
SING LIKE A JEWISH CANTOR.

Chapter Twenty-Seven

With the advent of television, in the late forties, we in Hollywood, along with the rest of the country, encountered the biggest novelty that ever hit the world. I, of course, knew the broadcasters were using movies on television, and I thought I would expand my operation and do some work for television.

I had an idea of doing movie star interviews, making use of a device that would allow local interviewers at television stations anywhere appear as if they were actually speaking one-to-one with the stars. It worked like this: the show opened with a scene of a star picking up a telephone, saying, "Hello, this is so-and-so, who's calling?" Then the star waited for ten seconds. We would supply a little script for the local station. The local announcer — anywhere in the world — could say, "Hello [star], this is [local interviewer] calling from XYZ Television. We want to interview you for our television show."

Next, the star would answer, "Oh yes, I'm glad you called, I've been waiting for your call, that's why I've had the phone sitting nearby." The star would continue to talk and tell about how he or she was taking the call in the living room, or out by the swimming pool, or "You just happened to catch me while I'm up in Las Vegas, having a holiday here at the Flamingo Hotel," or whatever.

Then the star would say, "What would you like to know?" and pause for another ten seconds, or whatever was the precise time we figured out for the script. The star would appear to be listening to the phone, and that was when the local announcer would fill in time using the words from our script to say. "Well, look, Sam, or look, Betty, what are you doing up there in Las Vegas?"

The star would answer, "Oh, let me show you what I've been doing," and they would start talking about having gone to Boulder Dam, or having taken a train to the

ECT GEORGE
  PREPARE
LM
WOOD ON
INE.

Grand Canyon, or some such thing, and as they were talking about these various locations, we would have scenes of them shot in those locations.

The first movie star that I could get hold of to do this, at a time when all movie studios forbade any of their contract actors from appearing on television, was George Raft. Raft was a nice enough guy to offer to do this for me, and we filmed the first one, the first pilot show, with him around his swimming pool with a whole bunch of pretty girls.

With that film shot I went back to New York and showed it to the president of CBS television, a man named Jack van Volkenberg, and he said, "Let's get an announcer to read the lines for this thing, the insert lines, to talk to George Raft."

"You don't need an announcer, Jack," I said, "anybody can do this. You sit down there, and you ask George Raft the questions."

We had a projector in his office, so we turned it on and Raft came out on the screen and you could hear a phone ringing. He left a group of girls and walked over to a table in his garden and picked up the ringing phone and said, "Hello, George Raft speaking." I touched Jack van Volkenberg and I pointed to the line. He said, "Hello, George, this is Jack van Volkenberg in New York."

Raft answered, "Oh yes — I'm glad to hear from you." The cue was perfect. Jack looked at this film and he flipped. I sold the series to CBS thanks to George Raft being bold enough to buck the power of the movie studios' prejudice against television.

The series ran for twenty-six episodes, and don't think it wasn't a problem to find twenty-six stars who would go on television and buck the movie studios' ban. Roddy McDowall was another who agreed to do the show. Rhonda Fleming, Jane Wyatt, Jack Carson, Jack Oakie, Virginia Bruce, Ilona Massey, and Buster Keaton were some of the others I persuaded to go on TV.

Now, more than forty years later, I hope to revive those early shows, update them with those who are still alive, and resell them as the first TV shows that broke the ice to get film stars to appear. Just another bit of show business history.

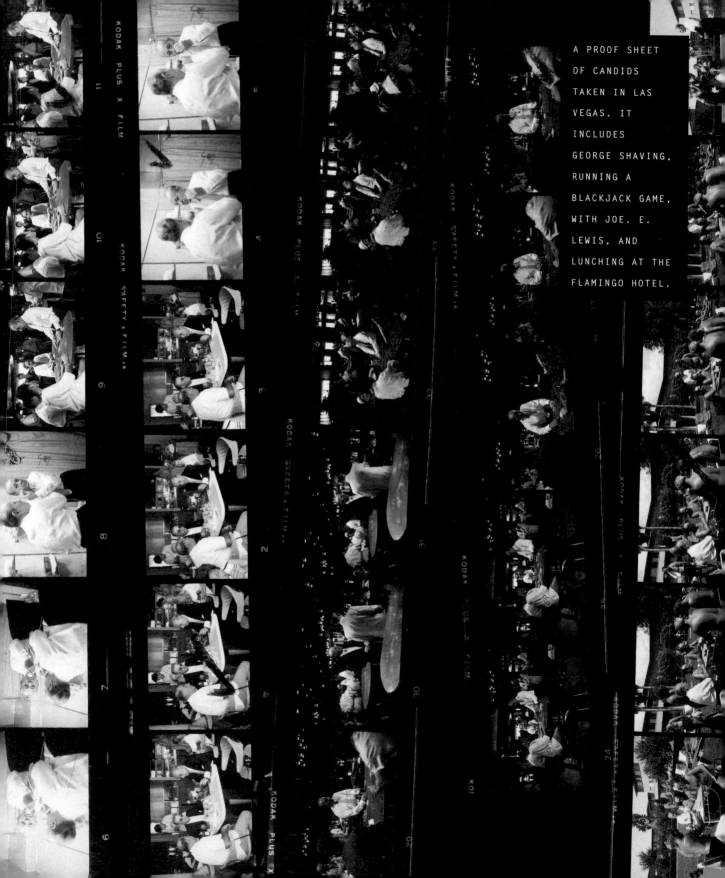

A PROOF SHEET OF CANDIDS TAKEN IN LAS VEGAS. IT INCLUDES GEORGE SHAVING, RUNNING A BLACKJACK GAME, WITH JOE. E. LEWIS, AND LUNCHING AT THE FLAMINGO HOTEL.

Chapter Twenty-Eight

I n the early 1950s, there was a group in Hollywood called the Hollywood Stereo Club. These were the movie stars who used to play around with shooting their own pictures, their home snapshots, in 3-D. There was a popular camera at that time called the Stereo Realist and it was the favorite of the shooters. Harold Lloyd was president of the Stereo Club, and among the members were people like Joan Crawford, Dick Powell, Ronald Colman, and Art Linkletter.

Harold Lloyd used to take a lot of cheesecake girlie pictures. That was his main interest in photography, to get undressed girls to pose for him. He had a huge collection of 3-D photographs of nudes and seminudes. The way he found his models was to go around and find amateur actresses and pay them for posing for him. One of the rooms in his house was a studio and was completely devoted to his 3-D photography.

In Hollywood, there was a place for young starlets and wannabes called the Studio Club. It was run by the YWCA as a boarding house of sorts for girls who were trying to make their way into show business.

At one time, Marilyn Monroe lived there, as did an actress named Louise Allbritton and a few others whose names elude me.

I had once done a photo layout on the Studio Club for the *Saturday Evening Post*, and as a result, many of the girls who resided there would drop into my office since it was on the way to Hollywood or Sunset boulevards.

From time to time I would hire some of them as models or secretaries as I was constantly losing my girls to better paying jobs.

Harold Lloyd heard that all the young girls from the Hollywood Studio Club used to come by my office regularly looking for modeling work. Since no men had access to the Studio Club roster, or were allowed to hang around the club to try to meet the girls, Harold used to hang around my office in hopes that he would meet all these young and hopeful movie starlets.

He found several of his models for his 3-D pictures from these Studio Club girls as well as from others who used to drop in. But while sitting around waiting, he and I would talk for hours on end about the early days of Hollywood and how he got started in the movies. He told me about his famous clock scene in *Safety Last* and how he lost three fingers in a bomb accident. He even showed me his ungloved hand. He usually wore a black glove with false fingers to mask his own missing ones.

Even though he was one of the richest men in Beverly Hills, he was just an ordinary guy when you got to know him. His interest in stereo photography was very great. I believe that he and his Stereo Club did more to promote 3-D photography than anyone.

HAROLD LLOYD (*RIGHT*) WAS RELUCTANT TO POSE FOR PICTURES BECAUSE
PART OF HIS HAND WAS BLOWN OFF IN AN ACCIDENT.
WHEN I PHOTOGRAPHED LLOYD AT NBC WITH COMEDIAN VICTOR
MOORE, HE KEPT HIS HAND HIDDEN IN A POCKET.

Chapter Twenty-Nine

During the early days of radio, there was a famous personality on the air called Professor Quiz. Nobody knew who this man was — you could ask him any question, and he had an answer for it. His identity was kept a complete secret from the audience and the public. The key to the publicity about him was to keep him a total mystery; nobody would know who Professor Quiz was.

Arthur Godfrey was the announcer on the "Professor Quiz Show." I was working for *Radio Guide* magazine at the time, and my editor there said, "Gee, if we could find out who Professor Quiz is, that would be a feather in our cap." Now, Arthur Godfrey had just been in an item in the columns because he had taken up flying lessons at Floyd Bennett Field, outside of New York, on the other end of Brooklyn. I decided I needed to get to know Godfrey, and through him, I would be able to find out the real name of Professor Quiz.

When Godfrey earned his pilot's license, I made an appointment to go to Floyd Bennett Field with him, and maybe go flying with him to do a picture layout.

Godfrey and I went flying in his little single-engine open-cockpit plane, like a Waco, or an Aircoup, or whatever it was that he had. He sat in the back, and I sat up in the front. He asked me if I had ever done any flying before, and I told him I had, up in Massachusetts when I worked for the *Worcester Telegram and Gazette*, I did some aerial shots for them, news pictures and shots of Holy Cross college football games.

Godfrey yelled at me, "Well, I'm going to fly like you've never flown before." I wondered, "What the hell is he up to now?" Well, he had decided that he was going to "crack my lunch."

He did wing-overs, barrel rolls, and loops, and everything possible. I had never experienced a loop-the-loop until that flight. There I was with my camera, in an

open-cockpit plane, and I had to finally change the film. I had run out of film because some of the cameras I had only took eight exposures at that time, instead of thirty-six like you get today with a 35mm.

I was looking inside the plane and doing what I had to do to change the film and not realizing whatever the plane was doing. Finally, over the ocean, I had some paper from the film wrapping in my hand and I was just going to throw it out of the plane. I looked down over the side of the plane and commented, "Where is the ground?" I did not see any ground. All I saw was a cloud down there. I looked up and there was the earth. I didn't even know we were flying upside down. But whatever Arthur did, he could not make me lose my lunch, and he did wing-overs, he did loops, he did a barrel roll, he did everything, and I never got really sick, and he said that I was the most disappointing passenger he had ever had in his life.

It was disappointing for me too because he would not tell me who Professor Quiz was.

Not much later, I was in a Manhattan office building and got in the down elevator, and I heard the voice of a man talking to someone else. He was a well-dressed, sort of stout, middle-aged man — kind of "spiffy" — wearing a sport coat and white flannel pants. I said to myself, "That's Professor Quiz! That voice, I know." It had become a project to me, I had to find out who this guy was. And this voice in the elevator sounded like just like him.

I was in position to get out of the elevator first; he was behind me. Outside on the sidewalk I waited for this guy to come out and got my little 35mm camera ready, and when he walked out of the building, I shot him.

I did not go over to the guy and ask him if it was okay, but I got him walking out of the building. Then I went to Arthur Godfrey, and said, "You wouldn't tell me who Professor Quiz was, but now I've got a picture of him." I didn't want to ask, "Is this Professor Quiz?" because then he would just say, "No." So I said, "I've got a picture of him and boy, you didn't have to tell me."

Then I showed Arthur the picture and he said, "How the hell did you get that?" That irritated reaction made me sure I had the right guy and we published it in *Radio Guide*, "Professor Quiz Unmasked!"

FLEDGLING PILOT
GODFREY DEMONSTRATES
HOW THE FLAPS
ON THE WING MOVE.

Chapter Thirty

Before I left New York, when I was working for radio station WHN, Major Bowes aired his "Amateur Hour" there, before it went to the NBC coast-to-coast network. Many of the amateur performers were not auditioned in advance, they just came up a couple of hours before the show to audition, and then, if the Major liked them, he would put them on the show. I was working at the reception desk one day taking down the names of all the applicants. Along came a thin, scrawny kid, who looked like a skeleton with flesh, and he had scars on his neck and his face. He looked like somebody had tried to cut his head off.

I looked at him and I said "Yes, what's your name?"

"My name is Frank Sinatra," was the reply.

I said, "Gee, Sinatra? Are you related to a band leader I knew in Boston named Ray Sinatra?"

"Evidently," he told me. "We're all Sicilians, the Sinatras. The family is all Sicilian, and if he's a Sinatra, then he must be a cousin."

"What's your name?" he then asked me.

I told him, "My name's Gene Lester." He thought for a moment.

"Are you the Gene Lester who sings on this radio station?"

I said, "Yes," and started to smile.

And he went on, "Gee, I wish I had a job like yours. I wish I could have a job singing on the radio."

I thought nothing of it at the time. But later, when Frank was such a huge star, I never forgot that he was the only guy who ever said to me, "Gee, I wish I had a job like yours!"

Working as a free-lance photographer in Hollywood in the old days was sort of

like being in a closed group, like a family. Because I knew so many of the stars and publicists and producers, rather than scrounging around looking for clients, my work usually came from referrals and contacts.

That is how the publicist George Evans happened to call me up one day and ask me to go out to the Pasadena Railroad Station and photograph the arrival on the Coast of this kid singer, Frank Sinatra.

George said to me, "Look, I hired a bunch of broads — high school kids — I gave them a buck a piece to come out and swoon and scream and yell when he gets off the train, so get a shot of that, will you?"

I said, "Fine," and went out to Pasadena to cover the arrival. Frank got off the train, and I took a whole series of pictures of him. He got in amongst all these girls and he signed autograph books and he was handing them out to the girls but because I am so short, I was unable to shoot over the heads of people and get a good view of Frank.

"Let's get a ladder for Frank so I can see him over the heads of the people and give me one of those baggage carts," I told the publicity people. I got up on the baggage cart and shot the pictures of Frank up above the girls.

The whole thing was a screaming mess. Yes, a couple of people from RKO came out and greeted him, because he was arriving for his first movie, a film called *Higher and Higher*. But the screaming kids were all phonies. In fact they were even phonies at the New York Paramount when the publicity came out that girls started fainting in the aisles supposedly because this guy was so great. George Evans paid them off. He told them to start screaming, and when girls heard others scream, girls who were not paid off, who were in the crowd as part of the regular audience, would join in the melee. That is exactly what happened, wherever they went. Evans and his crew had plants scattered throughout the audiences to start yelling and screaming, and the kids around those kids would start yelling and screaming too.

That whole thing was such a phony bit. When Kitty Kelley did her life story of Sinatra, she wrote that five thousand screaming girls met him at the Pasadena Railroad Station. There were not even fifty girls. I know because I was there and took pictures of that whole group. When the Pasadena arrival event was all over and when those hired girls who made such a big to-do, screaming, "We want his autograph; hey, don't let him go!" finished their act after tearing at his sleeves and everything — and finally the police got him away — I was on that baggage cart, packing my cameras into my case. A bunch of the girls came over to me and asked, "Who was that guy?" They had been paid to scream when a guy got off the train. They had no idea who he was.

SINATRA HITS HOLLYWOOD.

PUBLICITY PICTURES
OF EARLY SINATRA
DURING A RECORDING
SESSION.

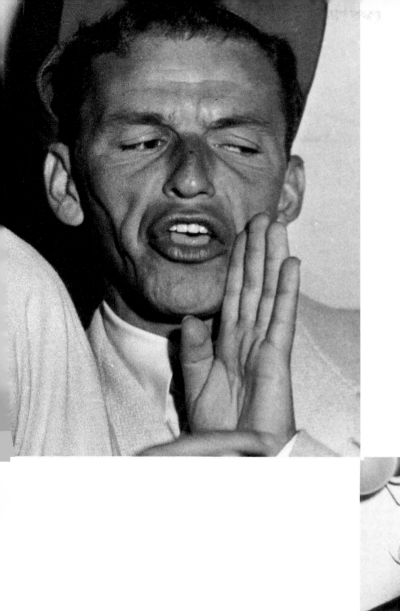

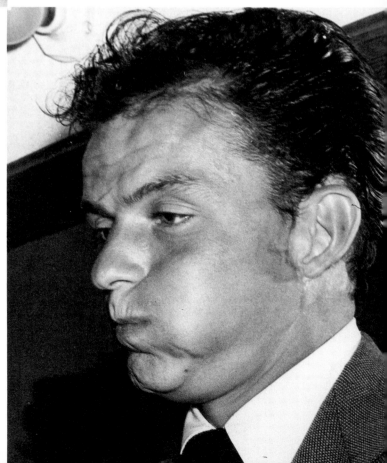

Chapter Thirty-One

Bob Hope had an air about him that you felt you knew this guy well from the first five minutes that you were with him. Hope was one of the first guys in radio to move to California. He went to work at Paramount in 1938 and made a picture in which he first sang "Thanks for the Memory."

I did a picture layout on Bob for *Radio Guide* at that time. He had some big dogs, and he used to ride his bike all around Toluca Lake, where he lived. That was his exercise. I spent a day with Bob there at the Toluca Lake house in the San Fernando Valley. He still had his radio show, and that same afternoon some of the guys who wrote the show for him came over.

He used to take their paychecks and make them up into paper airplanes. Then he would stand up at the top of the stairway and take the paper airplanes and say, "Oh, this is for you," and he would fly the check down to the waiting writers. This was really an insult to the writers. But to Bob it was his way of having fun.

I had the good fortune of being selected from all the photographers to travel with the Hollywood Victory Caravan during the early days of World War II. This was a month-long train trip around the United States with stopovers in major cities where forty-odd stars headed by Bob Hope and Bing Crosby would put on performances in an effort to sell war bonds. This first Victory Caravan was one of the biggest money-makers for the war effort ever staged by one group.

Bob and Bing were not on the initial leg of the trip, but flew in when the train arrived in Washington for the first performance, which was to be attended by Eleanor Roosevelt. I believe FDR was away in Yalta at the time.

That evening, I was backstage roaming from dressing room to dressing room catching candid shots of the performers being made up for the show — Cary Grant,

GARLAND
MPLATES
TO DO
BOB'S HAIR
TAGE.

Groucho Marx, Laurel and Hardy, Desi Arnaz, James Cagney, Claudette Colbert, Olivia de Havilland, Joan Bennett, Eleanor Powell, and many more. In Hope's dressing room I happened to catch him in his underwear getting ready to put on his evening clothes. So I shot the picture. Hope made no comment at the time because he knew me and that I wouldn't release a picture that showed him in a bad light.

One day about a year later, Bing Crosby was in my office on Vine Street and he saw the picture of Bob Hope in underwear up on the wall. The guys in the lab had just stuck it up as a crazy shot. Crosby took it off the wall and back with him to the NBC studios. During the prebroadcast warmup for Bob's show, when the stars come out and talk to the audience and tell them what they are supposed to do and can expect during the show, Bing came out and started talking to the audience about Hope. Suddenly, Bing picked up that picture of Bob in his underwear that he had taken from my studio, and he showed it to the audience.

Bob was on the sidelines and he saw Bing holding something up. Then he saw what it was. He ran out and he tried to grab the picture. Bing took it and skooned it out to the audience; let it spin through the air and wherever it landed everybody made a grab for the picture — tearing it to shreds grabbing for it.

As part of their routine that night Bing and Bob had this great big to-do over that photograph. Bob told me later that he went down into the audience to retrieve the pieces, but the shreds weren't worth saving. I later made a new print and gave it to Bob.

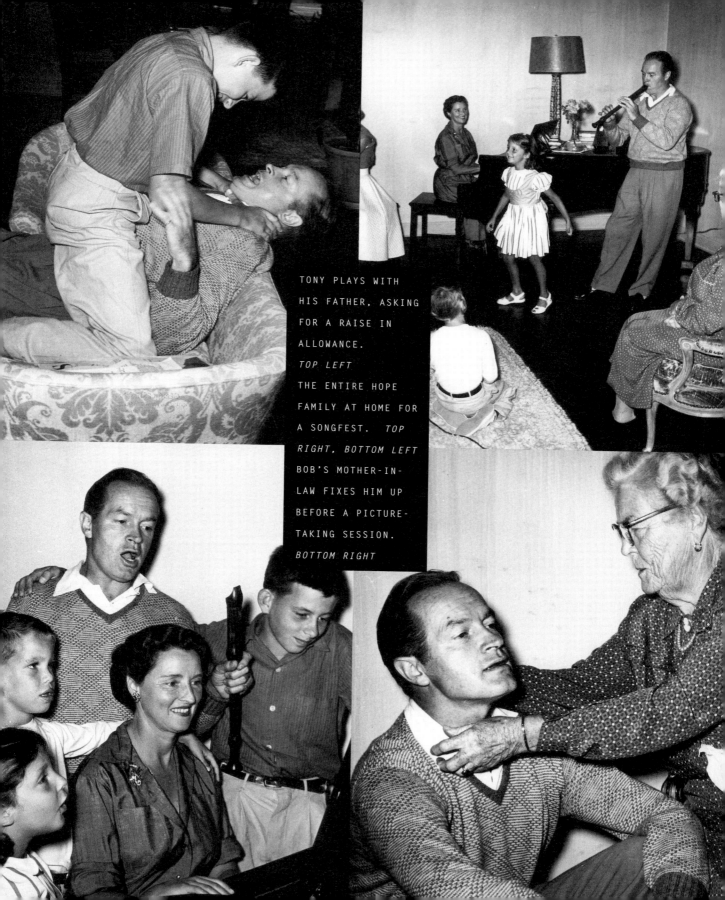

TONY PLAYS WITH HIS FATHER, ASKING FOR A RAISE IN ALLOWANCE. *TOP LEFT* THE ENTIRE HOPE FAMILY AT HOME FOR A SONGFEST. *TOP RIGHT, BOTTOM LEFT* BOB'S MOTHER-IN-LAW FIXES HIM UP BEFORE A PICTURE-TAKING SESSION. *BOTTOM RIGHT*

BOB AND HIS DOG

IN 1938.

WHEN THE HOLLYWOOD PRESS PHOTOGRAPHERS
VOTED RITA HAYWORTH AND BOB HOPE
AS THE MOST COOPERATIVE STARS, AWARDS WERE
PRESENTED ON THE CECIL B. DE MILLE
"LUX RADIO THEATER." BECAUSE OF MY RADIO
EXPERIENCE, I WAS SELECTED BY THE GROUP
TO DO THE PRESENTATION ON THE AIR.

Chapter Thirty-Two

John Wayne and William Holden signed to do a movie called *The Horse Soldiers*, a story about the Civil War cavalry. While they were doing that picture, I was doing promotion for a little camera company called Eumig, a German-Austrian firm that made both an 8mm and a 16mm movie camera. They wanted me to get stars to publicize their cameras.

When I brought a couple of those Eumig cameras to John Wayne's house, John was like an overgrown kid with a new toy. He was living in Encino in one of those fantastic homes with a driveway a quarter of a mile long crossing a hill and a field to get to the house. It was a beautiful estate.

We gave him some rolls of film, and he was having a ball, running around shooting, when the director, John Ford, showed up. Ford saw John Wayne running around with a camera, and he started directing Wayne, as if they were making a big picture — with a dinky little 8mm camera.

Then Ford grabbed the camera to take some pictures of Wayne to include in the footage. It was then that I started laughing.

"Here you both are," I said, "two of the biggest people in Hollywood, with the dinkiest camera you would ever want to hold in your hand. This is a nothing 8mm camera. They take the lousiest pictures in the world, I'm sure."

At that point, John Ford came over to me and he said, "Wait a minute, kid." He could be tough with that patch over his eye. He acted like a real tough Irishman who came out of the marines.

"I want you to know," he growled at me, "that I won an Academy Award with an 8mm camera. Do you remember during the war a film called *Fighting Lady*, about the aircraft carrier?"

JOHN WAYNE AND
WILLIAM HOLDEN
WITH HOME MOVIE
CAMERAS ON THE
SET OF *THE
HORSE SOLDIERS*.

"Yes," I was listening carefully, "I saw it. A great movie!"

"Do you realize," he lectured me, "that ninety percent of that movie was shot with an 8mm camera, by a bunch of guys who died doing it?"

"No," I said. "I never knew that. It never dawned on me." I was stunned.

"You speak with respect about an 8mm camera, kid," Ford said and walked away.

Chapter Thirty-Three

Jimmy Durante started out here in Hollywood in the revue, *Earl Carroll's Vanities*. He had broken up with Lew Clayton and Eddie Jackson, who had been his partners, and was doing a solo bit. At that time he was under contract to MGM and I was handling the Earl Carroll publicity photography and got to work quite a bit with Durante. He used to come out to my studio often, with the girls. We made a lot of pictures of him with the Earl Carroll girls in their sexy costumes.

The only way you could get a guy publicity in a show like that would be to surround him with girls. Mack Sennett used to do the same thing with his comedians in the early silent days, when he showcased the cross-eyed comedian Ben Turpin. Sennett's publicity staff once arranged for a picture of Turpin with a bunch of Mack Sennett bathing beauties, and Turpin was at the left end of the picture. When the magazine editors got the picture, they cut Ben Turpin out and just published the bathing beauties. So from then on, Mack Sennett said that every picture shot of the girls with Ben Turpin must show him in the middle of the girls, with all of them packed around him.

It was the same with Jimmy Durante. We used to shoot Jimmy with all the Earl Carroll girls surrounding him, or in some way he had to have something to do with the girls, so editors could not cut him out. We made sure Durante was part of the story of the picture.

When I got an assignment to do Durante's life story for the *Saturday Evening Post* (in the early fifties), it was at a time when he was working at Universal in some movie. The day I arrived on the set, Jimmy was playing a milkman in the picture. This particular scene took a few days to shoot and it showed Jimmy running around without his pants on. He was in his shirttails and his undershorts and socks.

I wanted to get this picture of him with no pants on, so I said, "Jimmy, let's get

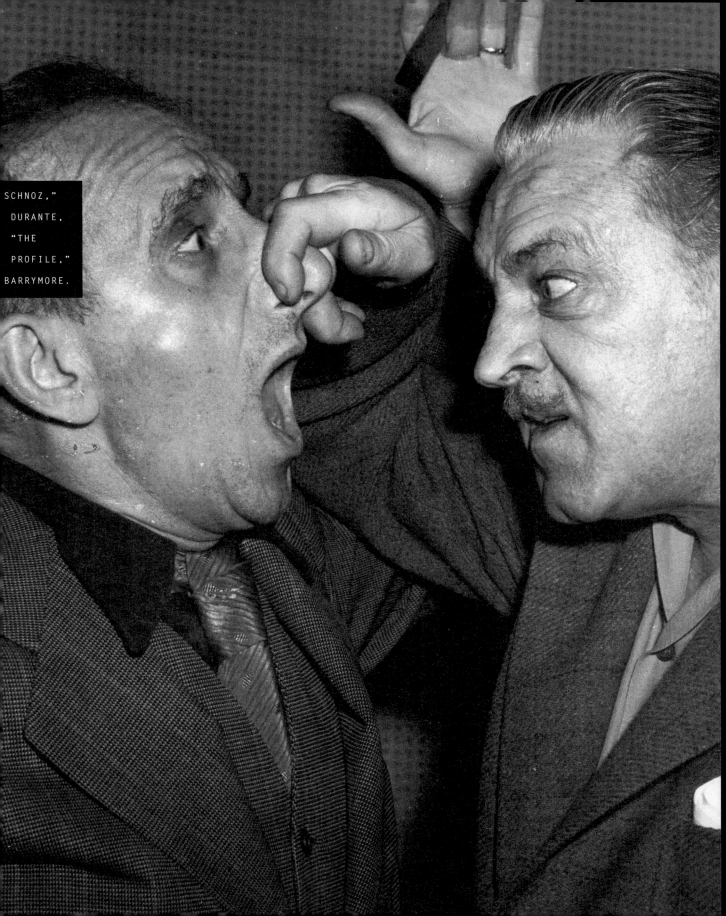

a pair of pants from wardrobe and just have them dangling around your ankles, hanging down there like you've just dropped your pants. It would look funnier than your being there with no pants on. The extra pants, around your ankles, would make the picture look funnier."

He agreed, but complained, saying, "The dressing room is half a mile down the Universal lot." We were way out on a hill on a stage at the fringes of the lot. "It would take us an hour to get a pair of pants," he said. And he was right.

So I took my pants off and I told Jimmy to get into them and let them dangle around his ankles. There was Jimmy, with no pants on, and my pants around his ankles. There I was with no pants on, shooting a picture layout of Jimmy. My God, the things I do for my editors!

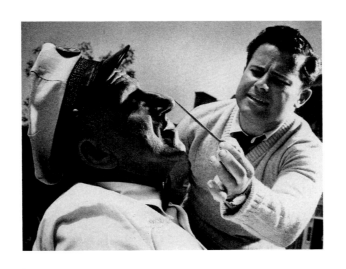

FRANK WESTMORE, THE MAKEUP MAN ON
THE MILKMAN, GIVES SPECIAL ATTENTION
TO THE FAMOUS DURANTE NOSE.

Chapter Thirty-Four

When I first landed in Hollywood, I was supposed to cover all the radio shows that originated on the West Coast. *Radio Guide* used to send me around to appear on some of those shows, too, as their singing photographer. The first show I ever did in Hollywood for the magazine was the "George Jessel Show." They booked a movie star guest that day too, a girl who was about eighteen or nineteen at the time, named Betty Grable.

Betty Grable was then was married to Jackie Coogan. He had costarred with Charlie Chaplin in *The Kid* when he was five years old. But now he was a grown man, a giant of a man, about six feet two or so. He was solid too; he looked like a wrestler. He was such a big bruiser and was married to this dainty little girl.

Betty Grable was supposed to sing a song on the Jessel show. I was supposed to sing too. Once we got the show all lined up and boxed in to know the timing on everything, we realized there was no time for both of us to sing a separate song. So the producers decided that we would do a duet together. I was to sing "The Lady Is a Tramp," and she was to join in.

Betty was very nice about it. A lot of stars would have said, "Hey — get this guy out of here. I'm the star." But Jessel, whose show was not well known at the time, needed publicity in *Radio Guide* and he would have turned around if Betty Grable had complained and said, "Grable, get off the show."

But she did not complain when they put us together, and we ended up good friends. We did the "Tramp" duet.

Later she and Jackie invited me to their place so I could shoot a picture layout of the two of them at home, in their little dinky apartment. They were living in Santa Monica at the beach, and I was the first one to shoot Jackie Coogan and Betty Grable at

home. Through the years Betty and I remained friends. When she divorced Jackie, she started dating George Raft, whom I also knew well. Many's the time we sat together at restaurants and in nightclubs while I made like I wanted to steal Betty away from him. All in fun. Even later, when she married bandleader Harry James, I visited them at their ranch and brought out bicycles as gifts for their two daughters. I was very saddened on learning of Betty's death at an early age.

I HAD KNOWN BETTY
SINCE MY FIRST DAYS
IN HOLLYWOOD,
SO I TRIED TO
GRAB HER AWAY FROM
GEORGE RAFT.

BETTY ON A RADIO
SET WITH A
JAIL DOOR PROP.

Chapter Thirty-Five

When doing picture layouts of stars at home, I like to be thorough. I do not like to leave any phase of a star's home life untouched. It does not matter to me what the editor does with it later, but at least I then know I supply all the raw material, the grist for the mill.

When I was assigned to go out to Kirk Douglas's house, he was fairly newly married. His bride did not want to be in too many photographs, so I had to concentrate mostly on him and the business that he carried on in his house.

I shot him at his business office, and in the house, and having breakfast, and dinner, and shaving, and all that kind of stuff — all the intimacies of home life. When I was through, after several days of shooting, and I was leaving, he turned to me and he said, "You know, you're pretty damn thorough. You had me do everything but stand on my head."

"Oh, no," I replied, "How can I miss that? So let's go. Stand on your head."

He said, "You mean it?"

"You're damn right," I told him. "You brought it up."

"Yeah," he answered, "I can stand on my head. I can really do a good job standing on my head." He went out in the back yard and he started doing a couple of flip-flops, and he stood on his hands, and I got his picture.

These stars talked to me as a colleague. There was nothing demanding like, "Well, are you through?" Or, "What else do you want?" or anything like that. It was more like what Douglas said to me about standing on his head. We were working together to accomplish a job that needed to be done and we tried to make the most of it — to enjoy it.

DOUGLAS IN
BACKYARD,
G WHAT
S
RALLY.

That is why I shot pictures of Errol Flynn sitting on the john. Flynn had just come out of the shower and he said, "I've got to take a crap."

"Go ahead," I told him.

He said, "You don't have to leave."

"I don't want to hang around while you're stinking up the joint," was my answer. But instead, since I did have my Speed Graphic in my hand, I waited.

He sat down on the john with everything hanging out, and I flashed my camera. He did not care. He knew that I would not use the picture and that it probably would wind up on my dar room wall. It did wind up on my darkroom wall and eventually somebody swiped the picture and the negative, too.

KIRK DOUGLAS
AT HOME
AND AT WORK.

185

Chapter Thirty-Six

When Danny Thomas came out to Hollywood from his nightclub appearances in Chicago, he was signed to do a radio show in which he played a mailman. A girl from the advertising agency that sponsored the radio show called me and said, "We just signed a new comedian and we have no pictures of him whatsoever. He does a nightclub act where he wears a hat and has a cigar in his mouth. We don't want that kind of stuff. We want anything that's crazy. Just do anything you want to do that's crazy. We'll send him to your studio the day after he arrives."

So Danny Thomas's first full day in Hollywood was spent at my studio. Danny came in and we sat and talked for the first hour or so. I did not know what to do with him. They told me anything funny.

We went into the studio, where I had just finished shooting a girl. Her lipstick was on the dressing table, and for some reason, I had a fright wig there, too. I think we had used it on Groucho Marx. There was also a piece of fabric that had a zebra skin design on it.

I said, "Danny, let's make you up with the fright wig and I'll use the girl's lipstick and paint your face up like a wild African native. We'll wrap you up in the zebra skin, and you wear the wig and we'll do some crazy pictures." I also had a furry little piece of rug in my studio that day. We took it and wrapped it around his waist, like a caveman. That was what I made him look like. I did a whole series of pictures of Danny doing all these crazy antics with this makeup.

Necessity is the mother of invention, as the saying goes. Those spur-of-the-moment photos of Danny Thomas appeared everywhere. The sponsor was so pleased that they also turned over other accounts to me.

Danny himself enjoyed the session and we became good friends. I recall one

incident when I was covering a story at the Desert Inn in Las Vegas. Danny came to Vegas to open at the Inn and we bumped into each other in the dining room. He asked, "Gene, have you had dinner yet?" When I answered that I hadn't, he insisted, "Please sit down and have dinner with me. I can't stand eating alone. I must have company to talk to." I had dinner with him and even worked him into my picture-layout assignment, which pleased both him and my picture editor.

HIS RADIO SPONSOR SET UP THE DATE
FOR "CRAZY" PICTURES ONLY.

Chapter Thirty-Seven

During the late twenties and the early thirties, Rudy Vallee was probably one of the most famous entertainers in the world. Rudy was the crooner that all the girls swooned over.

Rudy used to have a lodge in Maine. He is a New Englander like I am, from further north. During the summer when he had days off, he would have his chauffeur drive him up to his lodge from New York City. The trip was a good day's long drive on the roads then; there were no freeways like now. Rudy would leave New York about eight o'clock in the morning; he would arrive in Worcester about noon, just in time for lunch. He had a favorite restaurant, Putnam & Thurston's, there in downtown Worcester. We used to ask the owner of the place to call us local photographers when any celebrity ever came into Worcester and ate there.

I went out to wait for his arrival one time and he had a new singer with him named Alice Faye. He was taking her up to the lodge. I went in and introduced myself to Rudy and he asked me to come and have lunch with them.

This was the very first time a star had ever asked me to do anything with him, and I said, "No, I already ate my lunch, and thank you, but I'll wait outside." Finally, he came out and he and Alice stood alongside this big limousine that they had driven up in. I was using a Graflex camera, and I was looking up at the sky, checking the light and then I was looking at him.

We had no exposure meters in those days. Everything was guess. You had to know what speed your film was. While I was estimating the light, Rudy yelled over to me, "A fiftieth at eight!"

"Gee, that's right," I said. "A fiftieth at eight is what I would have estimated this to be." I shot it at that setting and got a great picture.

WITH ONE
E CAMERAS
HIS
SIVE
CTION.

A few years went by and I was down in New York at the Astor Hotel where Rudy was playing, and was assigned to take some pictures of him on the bandstand with his group: Rudy Vallee's Connecticut Yankees. I was in the club, getting my camera set, and he looked down at me from the bandstand and shouted, "A fiftieth at eight!" The setting was the same exposure with flashbulbs at night in that club as it was during the daytime up in Massachusetts those years back with the existing light.

Well, "a fiftieth at eight" became the byword between me and Rudy Vallee, and in New York I got to know him well. Rudy joined the radio migration out to the West Coast, and moved into a house on Hollywood Boulevard west of Laurel Canyon, where Hollywood winds up in the hills. I came out to shoot some pictures of him up there and again he said, "A fiftieth at eight!"

Rudy was quite a camera buff. That is why he could estimate exposures. He had a projection room up at that house, and he put in twin projectors so that he could put on movie shows for his friends. He was one of the first actors ever to get his own films from the studios in 16mm. I bought my own projector once I settled in Hollywood and Rudy would loan me his films so that I could put on private movie shows.

Every Sunday night, I would put on a show for my new Hollywood friends. Rudy would supply the feature and I would invite actors, publicity people I worked with, and other friends over. We did not have enough chairs for everyone, so I had them bring their own chairs, pillows, or seats from their car so they could sit comfortably on the floor.

One night we ran a picture featuring Tyrone Power and skater Sonja Henie with Rudy Vallee as supporting player. It contained songs by Irving Berlin. The film had run for about fifteen minutes and Rudy was just starting to sing in the film when he walked into the room, saw himself on the screen, moved over beside his screen image, and started to sing a duet with himself. The crowd watching was amazed at this. Rudy in person singing with Rudy on the screen. They applauded wildly when he finished.

To cap off the evening, during the changing of the reels Skitch Henderson played on my studio piano, Jackie Cooper played his drums which he had brought, Rudy had his saxophone and joined in, Ken Murray was there with his clarinet, and Larry Adler's brother, Jerry, played the harmonica. What a great show.

RUDY VALLEE JOINS CLAUDETTE
COLBERT AND RANDOLPH SCOTT ON AN ARMED
FORCES RADIO BROADCAST.

Chapter Thirty-Eight

One night I was at Ciro's and Greer Garson was there with a publicist named Harry Crocker, who was a scion of the Crocker family of San Francisco, the Crocker Bank founders. Harry Crocker was working in Hollywood as sort of a companion to stars. He was Charlie Chaplin's publicity man for a while, and Greer Garson and Harry were sitting at a remote table in the back at Ciro's. As was often the case with stars out on the town, I was invited to sit down and talk with them. I had finished taking pictures of the stars in the club that evening, and was just hanging around waiting to see if any other things would happen or any other stars would show up.

While I was at her table, Greer heard a song; the band was playing one that was very dear to her, a World War II song — "A Nightingale Sang in Berkeley Square." At that moment, Greer Garson — and this was just unbelievable from the image I had of her — reached into her purse, one of these evening purses with rhinestones and all that sort of stuff, and took out a little harmonica about an inch or an inch and a half long. It was the kind that some of those harmonica players would keep in their mouths and then all of a sudden start playing and the audience would wonder, "Where did that come from?" She put it in her mouth, and the next thing I knew, she was playing the song with them, on that tiny harmonica. My eyes just popped out of my head. I could not believe that this English woman who was almost queenly in her image, would pull out a dinky little harmonica and start playing it.

Chapter Thirty-Nine

We Hollywood photographers who were considered to be the inner circle — there were about ten of us — would have pretty much free rein at the nightclubs, like Ciro's and Mocambo, and the restaurants like La Rue and Romanoff's and Chasen's. We could walk in with our cameras and just hang around, or we would be given a table off to the side of the main room, or else the club would have a special place in the foyer where the cameramen could all congregate and just wait for stars to show up.

One evening, we were waiting for stars to show up at Ciro's when in walks Mickey Rooney with this gorgeous girl. Mickey was even shorter than I am, and I am only five feet, five and a half inches. I think Mickey was only about five feet. This girl must have been about five seven or five nine, something like that. We all wondered who she was, and he introduced us to her as his wife.

That news woke us up. All of us cameramen grabbed our cameras and started popping bulbs all over the place.

She was a quiet, unassuming girl, pretty and statuesque for her age. I imagine she was nineteen or twenty. It was Ava Gardner.

Years later, I was assigned to do a picture story about her, and by then she had broken up with Rooney. She was then going with a radio actor turned movie star, Howard Duff. I wanted desperately to get some pictures of Ava in a bathing suit, but she kept turning me down and I could not figure out why. She would do many other pictures but not in swimsuits. Most of the stars enjoyed showing themselves off in the fan magazines.

I decided that somehow I was going to work out something that would get her into a bathing suit. Every time I did a layout for a magazine like *Look* or *Life* or the

GARDNER
ES SHE CAN
A BIKE AND
BEAUTIFUL AT
SAME TIME.

Saturday Evening Post, I liked to inject a little bit of cheesecake — especially when it involved a very beautiful young girl like Ava.

I was at her place shooting pictures, the session was going very well, she was doing all the normal things that a girl does living as a single woman in her home or apartment. But I was scheming to get her to show off more of herself. She had a bicycle in her backyard, and I wanted to get a shot of her riding a bike. She got on the bike in her skirt.

"No way," I told her, "would you ride a bike wearing a long skirt?" I suggested that she might just as well put on shorts. I figured if I could not get her in a bathing suit, I would get her in shorts and a sweater, or a blouse.

But Ava absolutely refused to put on shorts. I could not figure this out. What the heck was wrong with this girl. Finally she confessed to me that she had a big scar — there was a big piece of flesh missing from her thigh. She was absolutely and totally embarrassed about showing that.

"Look," I explained to her, "there's no problem. If I don't photograph you from a certain angle, if you bend one knee around, in front of the other, it would hide it."

"Oh, you can do that?" She was surprised and finally agreed to let me shoot her in the shorts. After she saw the prints, Ava came over and threw her arms around me and said, "Oh, Gene. You made me feel so good. You made me feel like there was nothing wrong with me." This had been the bane of her existence, worrying about all the fan magazines, and the cheesecake shots — because every starlet, every young pretty star had to do cheesecake.

AVA GARDNER AND PETER LAWFORD.

Chapter Forty

Years ago, whenever ships arrived in New York harbor, it was the custom for a tugboat or a tender carrying the press to go out when the ship was about an hour away from docking. By the time the liner was just entering the outlying portions of New York Harbor, all the news photographers and reporters would be on board, so that they would have an hour with any celebrity who happened to be on the ship for interviews and pictures.

Back in the twenties, there was a photographer on the New York *Daily News* named Izzie Kaplan. Kaplan was one of the men sent out into the harbor on a particular morning because Queen Marie of Rumania was landing on the *Ile de France*. Queen Marie happened to be the youngest member of royalty in the entire European scene. She was in her middle or late twenties at the time, and she was a very attractive woman.

When the photographers all lined up to get pictures of Queen Marie on board, Izzie Kaplan asked her to sit up on the rail. While waiting for the Queen to show up for this photo opportunity, the men had their cameras all set up on deck. They had lunch boxes with them, because they never knew how long the ship was going to be out in the harbor. So they always carried their lunch with them. Izzie Kaplan used to carry his sandwich, a corned beef sandwich from a New York deli, and a big hunk of cheesecake, that New York style of creamy cheesecake.

Before the Queen came out, the guys started munching on their food. Izzie had a hunk of cheesecake in his hand, and the Queen showed up, and they asked her to sit up on the deck rail. She sat up there, and the women wore high-laced shoes at the time. They did not look too attractive. One of the photographers asked her to raise her skirt above the shoes. I do not know whether Izzie did or one of the other New York photographers.

She raised her skirt up to her knees. This was horrifying in those days. Here was the Queen, showing her knees in a photograph. Izzie Kaplan had this hunk of cheesecake in his hand, and he looked at the Queen's knees, and he said, "This is better than cheesecake!"

He put down his cheesecake and started shooting pictures. From that point on, every time a girl showed her legs or more, it was called "cheesecake."

HERE I AM SETTING UP THE COVER SHOT OF ANNETTE FUNICELLO'S ALBUM *MUSCLE BEACH PARTY*. THE MAN ON THE LEFT IS PETER LUPUS, LATER OF "MISSION IMPOSSIBLE" FAME.

SHOOTING THE *EARL CARROLL VANITIES* GAVE ME A
CONSTANT SUPPLY OF CHEESECAKE. I WAS THE
ONLY MAN ALLOWED IN THE GIRLS' DRESSING
ROOM, AND I WORKED HARD TO FILL THE DEMAND
THAT THE SHOW RECEIVED FROM NEWSPAPERS AND
MAGAZINES FOR CHEESECAKE PICTURES.

When Hollywood Was Fun

Back in the old days — in the thirties, forties, and fifties — I would do the rounds of nightclubs until two in the morning, to see what movie stars were out and who was dating whom. That is how we early Hollywood paparazzi operated.

We would go into the nightclubs and we got to know all the maitre d's, and all the owners. There was Ciro's and there was the Mocambo, those were two of the biggies. Then there were also restaurants, famous restaurants where stars would eat dinner, like the Brown Derby, and there was the big La Rue's Restaurant which was owned by the owner of *The Hollywood Reporter*.

We would just stand there, or we would take a table way off on the side and get a free drink. We were well known in all these places. Sometimes a star would say, "Why don't you sit over here with us? We'll talk." But if they wanted their privacy, I would not bother them and I certainly never took pictures of them if they said no.

First of all, we did not have as good lenses as photographers use today. If we saw a Fergie nude on a beach a thousand feet away, we had no lens that could cover that distance. Today they have amazing equipment. But in the thirties and forties, people did not spend hundreds of dollars for cameras. When we photographers sold a candid picture made in a nightclub or restaurant, invariably we earned only three to ten dollars for each shot. Today the magazines and tabloids pay a hundred thousand dollars for a picture because Fergie's has no clothes on at an island somewhere in the south of France.

Sometimes I get a little jealous of these new guys and their price tags for pictures, but then again I think, "Who needs it?" I was lucky enough to enjoy real relationships with the stars I photographed.

In Hollywood today, too many people working in the movie business feel as if movie stars are in a separate class. All these paparazzi who run around today, if they would see a Clark Gable, they would call him Mr. Gable, and a Jimmy Stewart, they would say Mr. Stewart. We never worked on that basis. It was always Jimmy, it was always Gary, it was Cary Grant by the first name. Or Charlton Heston. I never called him Charlton or Mr. Heston. It was always Chuck.

When I was working in Hollywood, that was always the way we operated. It was always a sort of an intimacy, and a friendliness. But there was still a businesslike attitude involved too because these people were under the control of a studio and they were told by the studio heads how they must act and that publicity is an extremely important factor in the making of movies. The stars were told that they should cooperate, that they should — if the journalist treats them with respect — treat the journalist with equal respect. Today that does not exist.

Stars back in the old days did not develop deep friendships with us photographers. They were sincere friendships, but they were not deep. The studios told them that that was the way they were supposed to do it and that was the way they felt they were supposed to do it, as thinking individuals. Today too many stars are not thinking individuals. Today Hollywood is full of people who are controlled by lawyers and accountants. They do whatever the lawyers and accountants say, or whatever their publicist says, and today the publicist says, "Stay away from all this press. Play hard to get. That's the way you get more publicity." Sure, you get more publicity in the scandal papers, but you do not get the publicity that is going to make the nice people around the country think how great you are.

Take, for example, Madonna coming out with the book called *Sex*. This may be great for her, and it may be what she wants to do, but it is not going to get her a lot of respect in this country. If movie stars, who in my day were thought of as gods and goddesses, want respect, they must play along in a respectful way. They can do whatever they want sexually, that is their business, what they do behind a closed door. Look at Rock Hudson; he was a big star for years. Everybody inside Hollywood talked about his being homosexual, but nobody reported it. Today, if a guy's a homosexual, Hollywood reporters say, "Great, wow, gee. He's a homosexual, let's make a big thing out of this guy." But it is nobody's business. If a girl and a guy are living together, that is their business, it was being done in the old days. But it is wrong to publicize the fact that all these stars are just living together, having babies out of wedlock. Because then why should the kids all over the world not mimic these big stars, people they consider gods and goddesses? If the stars can do it, the kids think they can, too.

Most Hollywood reporters in the thirties, forties, and fifties followed the rules for publicity set down by the studios. It would have ruined your career with the studios to report Hudson was a homosexual, or tell who was sleeping with whom, no question about it, because the studios controlled these people and the studios would frown on anything that would give Hollywood unfavorable publicity.

One of the reasons that I got along with the stars so well was that I wanted to make them look good. I never shot somebody to make them look bad, to give them a bad name. If somebody made a terrible face, I would not photograph it. If they made a funny face, I would ask if it was all right before I shot it.

A woman like Fanny Brice — Baby Snooks — was a funny-looking woman. She made funny faces, which were fine to photograph. But you do not take a girl like Joan Crawford and make her do funny stuff. Or you do not take a girl like Grace Kelly and show her picking her nose. It would absolutely destroy the illusion.

I have a picture of Claudette Colbert who was accidentally picking her nose at one time, and I absolutely refused to have that printed. She had her finger in her nose; it would leave a bad taste with the reader. If I am delineating a person, and trying to show their qualities, I do not take a picture of them picking their nose to show their qualities.

My job in Hollywood was to tell a story, to tell a story about a person, and to tell a story as I saw it. If I showed Joan Crawford scratching her rear end, I do not think that would have been a good shot.

How many stars are there today who can fill the shoes of Clark Gable or Tyrone Power or Spencer Tracy or any of the biggies from those great days of Hollywood. Even a Tom Cruise today, who is one of the biggest stars, and who probably gets ten times the money Clark Gable got, does not have the stature that Clark Gable had in his day. He lacks the color, the manliness, the balls.

I do not think Madonna or Meg Ryan or Sharon Stone, for example, will ever enjoy the stature of a Grace Kelly or a Judy Garland or a Bette Davis.

Society changed, the public changed. Movies and stars started to change when censorship ended. With the advent of these porno movies and adult films, the major studios are putting things on the screens today not because they have value for story telling, but they have shock value.

The people who made movies in the thirties, forties, and fifties came from a society that had heart. They had something in their heads that told them what was warm and good, and what people wanted to see. Today few producers have heart like they did back then. One picture came out with some heart, *Driving Miss Daisy*, without a foul word in it and it won all the Academy Awards. Why not make more movies like that? Why do they have to show a guy and a girl walk into a bedroom, take their clothes off, then get in bed. Usually they do not show them actually engaged in sexual intercourse, but they show them in the positions where they would be doing it. So they might as well show the whole thing happening. Why do they need this on the screen?

In the old days the actors would go through a door and shut it and the film would fade out, and you knew what was happening. That made sex mysterious. That made the sex in your head, in the imagination of it. That made sex almost holy. Today, they do not make it holy, they make it a spectator sport.

We Hollywood photojournalists never tried to shoot anybody in the nude. The most nudity we would show would be cleavage, or maybe legs with a dress all the way up. I have a picture of Rita Hayworth dancing down the street in Beverly Hills, doing twirls and her dress is flying way up, but it is not flying high enough to show her crotch. Almost, but it definitely does not show. It is a sexy picture. You see Rita Hayworth doing this twirl with her beautiful legs, and her hair flying and everything. It was simply gorgeous.

People do not go around the streets showing their pubic hair. So why should it be shown it in the movies? We never went as far as making R-rated still pictures. Everything was PG. Sure, we always tried to get a little more. There is a certain amount of lasciviousness in everybody.

Once when I was assigned to photograph Maria Montez at her house, she came out of the bedroom with no clothes on to pose for me, saying, "Isn't my body beautiful? Shouldn't we show it to the world?"

I said, "If I took a picture of you like this, I'd get arrested." In those days, if you showed pubic hair, it was illegal.

"Put something on," I told her and she went back into her bedroom and put on a filmy peignoir. You could see right through the thing.

"We should have a picture of my figure," she insisted.

So I stood her in the window and shot a silhouette of her in the window where we could not see any detail, just the outline of her body black against the brightly lit

MARIA MONTEZ. UNCENSORED.

sunny window. Cheesecake of the forties and fifties was nothing like the cheesecake is today. Cheesecake is no longer cheesecake. Now it is crotch cake.

I got to know these people so well that if I wanted to get some guy or gal under a shower, they would just do it for me.

The stars trusted me. While doing a home layout of Mickey Rooney years ago, I asked him to do a shot in the shower. Without batting an eyelash, he stripped down and hopped into the shower while I shot a flash of him getting soaked. MGM, where he was under contract, demanded to look at the negatives. When they saw that the shower shot showed too much, they scratched the non-showable parts off. Just for the hell of it, I made a print showing the full length of Mickey with all the scratch marks. That picture was better than if I had shown the original. It was printable without question and caused lots of comment and attention.

Another incident worth noting was when I did a home layout of Zsa Zsa Gabor and her then husband, George Sanders. After getting a picture of him in undershorts while shaving in the bathroom, I suggested he get under the shower. He did as directed. Then when all six-feet-two of Sanders soaking wet came out of the shower, he look down at me and went into a tirade. "All you little bastards are dictators. Napoleon was short, Hitler was short. Now you, Gene Lester, order a sedate Englishman like me to strip down and pose in the altogether. You, too, are a dictator!" Then he laughed and patted my cheek with a wet hand. "I was only kidding."

Doing a picture layout of Rhonda Fleming. I said, "Rhonda I want you under the shower, singing. You know how people sing in the shower?"

"Fine," she responded. "How do you want me?"

All I wanted was a head shot. So she got into her swim suit with it slipped way down low, just enough to barely cover her nipples, and there she was in the shower. I did not need to hide in the bushes with a long lens. I worked with Hollywood and was a part of the business.

I worked in the business back in the days when Hollywood was fun.

THE HOLLYWOOD CARAVAN

WAS A CROSS-COUNTRY TRAIN

TRIP OF STARS WHO PERFORMED

FOR THE WAR EFFORT. HERE

THEY ARE LEAVING

LOS ANGELES IN 1942.

BEING WELCOMED BY ELEANOR ROOSEVELT
AT THE WHITE HOUSE; USING THE CLUB
CAR ON THE SPECIAL TRAIN AS A REHEARSAL
HALL (WITH AND WITHOUT INSTRUMENTS) AND
STRETCHING THEIR LEGS DURING
A STOP IN ALBUQUERQUE.

BING CROSBY WITHOUT HIS TOUPEE, REHEARSING
BACKSTAGE IN BOSTON AS PART OF THE VICTORY CARAVAN.

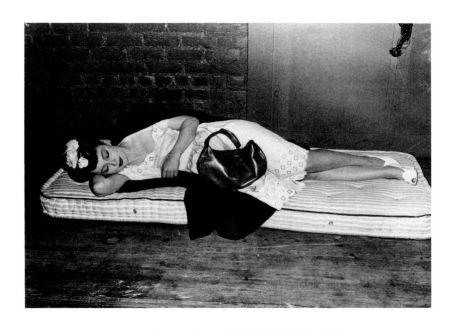

OLIVIA DE HAVILLAND CATCHES A NAP
BACKSTAGE DURING A VICTORY CARAVAN STOPOVER.

EDWARD G. ROBINSON POSING FOR SOME PUBLICITY
SHOTS FOR WARNER BROTHERS' *LITTLE CAESAR*.
THE PHOTOGRAPHERS WERE PART OF THE ACT, TO MAKE IT
APPEAR THAT TOUGH-GUY EDDIE WAS MEETING
THE PRESS IN HIS BATHTUB.

CLARK GABLE AND SPENCER TRACY, IN
BOOM TOWN, THEIR FIRST FILM TOGETHER.
IN THIS SERIES OF SHOTS, THEY
MANAGED TO COVER THEMSELVES, AS
WELL AS THE PHOTOGRAPHER, WITH MUD.

LUCILLE BALL,
WITH SON DESI,
JR., AND
PICKING UP
HER EMMY FROM
DON ADAMS FOR
THE "I LOVE
LUCY" SHOW.

WALT DISNEY SAID HE WOULD WEAR A MICKEY MOUSE HAT "ONLY OVER MY DEAD BODY." I CONVINCED HIS GRANDSON TO PUT THE HAT ON HIS GRANDFATHER AS HE READ THE LITTLE BOY A STORY. *INSET:* PICKING UP TRASH AT DISNEYLAND.

RODDY MC DOWALL BEING

MADE UP AS A CLOWN.

STEVE ALLEN
WORKING WITH ME
ON HIS BOOK *THE
QUESTION MAN*,
A CHARACTER HE
CREATED FOR
THE ORIGINAL
"TONIGHT SHOW."
TOP AT SUNSET
AND VINE
IN HOLLYWOOD.
BOTTOM

THE MARKINGS
ON THESE
PHOTOGRAPHS
WERE DONE BY
MAE WEST
HERSELF BEFORE
THEY WERE
RELEASED TO
THE PRESS AND
THE PUBLIC.

GENE LESTER
·DIRECTOR·